An Invincible Truth Volume II: The Most Honorable Elijah Muhammad's New Amsterdam News Articles Collection

Copyright 2018 Demetric Muhammad

All rights reserved. No part of this publication may be reproduced, distributed, or transmitted in any form or by any means, including photocopying, recording, or other electronic or mechanical methods, without the prior written permission of the publisher, except in the case of brief quotations embodied in critical reviews and certain other noncommercial uses permitted by copyright law. For permission requests, write to the publisher, addressed "Attention: Permissions Coordinator," at the address below.

ResearchMinister.Com
P.O. Box 993
Memphis, TN 38101
www.ResearchMinister.Com

Ordering Information:

Quantity sales. Special discounts are available on quantity purchases by corporations, associations, and others. For details, contact the publisher at the address above.

Printed in the Nation of Islam

ISBN-13: 978-0-9965156-5-8

DEDICATION

This book is dedicated to the Most Honorable Elijah Muhammad, the Honorable Minister Louis Farrakhan and the Nation of Islam

INTRODUCTION: STRONG MEDICINE

For the past 40 years, the Honorable Minister Louis Farrakhan has worked tirelessly to rebuild the work of the Most Honorable Elijah Muhammad. The Minister's tremendous work and global impact has caused a renewed interest in the basic and fundamental message and teachings of his beloved teacher -the Most Honorable and Honored Elijah Muhammad.

Thusly there is need for scholars, students, religious leaders, political leaders and the general public to have access to the pure and unfiltered message of Messenger Muhammad. For many years the writings and articles of the Most Honorable Elijah Muhammad have primarily been accessed through the series of books distributed under his name.

The Most Honorable Elijah Muhammad was not a writer of these books; his primary methodology for the distribution of his message was to teach lectures to mass audiences, to teach ministers and Nation of Islam officials who delivered his message throughout America and to publish articles in various newspapers.

Beginning in 1956 he began publishing a weekly series of articles in the Pittsburgh Courier newspaper. He would go on to publish articles in the New Amsterdam News, The Los Angeles Herald Dispatch, The Westchester Observer, The Chicago New Crusader and ultimately his own newspaper the Muhammad Speaks newspaper.

These were publications that comprised what was once known as the Negro Press. Most are no longer in production, and this has made accessing the original articles of Messenger Muhammad a challenge.

Yet accessing his original articles and writings is vitally necessary to be able to provide the clearest and truest presentation of his basic message and teachings as he originally published them.

The most popular books that bear his name were put together in a thematic and topical way first by John Ali, who served for a period of time as the Nation of Islam's National Secretary. Beginning in the 1980s and up until recent years others have also published Messenger Muhammad's writings in a thematic and topical way.

Both of these groups of publications contain content edits and the absence of citing the original source for the articles being presented. And based upon the very controversial nature of Messenger Muhammad's message it is important and necessary to present his message as close as possible to the way that he originally presented it.

So, the Invincible Truth series compiles and publishes as many of these original articles that we can find, with as much information about them that we can find. This is done without any content edits. Our effort is to give it to our readers the way Messenger Muhammad gave it to His readers. This obviously takes the form of a chronological arrangement and presentation of his writings.

This edition of the Invincible Truth series is devoted to preserving and presenting unedited the Most Honorable Elijah Muhammad's column titled The Islam World and The Islamic World that ran from 1957-1958 in the New Amsterdam News. This volume also includes a selection of the hard to find collection of articles that he published inside the Los Angeles Herald Dispatch and the Chicago Crusader and New Crusader. We have kept the emphasis utilized by bold typeface within certain articles as well as the very important content that He included inside of parenthesis. We have also attempted to maintain his spelling of various Proper Names and Places. As a student of the Honorable Minister Louis Farrakhan, I reflect in this regard on his noting that when the Most Honorable Elijah Muhammad used quotation marks and bold lettering, he was suggesting something of importance to the reader. So, we have made efforts to keep all such occurrences within the articles presented within this and all of the Invincible Truth volumes.

We believe that in addition to understanding the root of Minister Farrakhan's mind and teaching, these articles are also important as a necessary dose of strong medicine that needs to be injected into the current racial problems throughout America.

What the reader will find inside the articles of the Most Honorable Elijah Muhammad is unfiltered. It is not "politically correct." But neither was the teachings of any of the Prophets. The divine men and women of history all spoke truth that was deemed inconvenient and uncomfortable to many of their contemporaries. There is even a considerable amount of available literature devoted to the study and analysis of what scholars have labeled as the "hard sayings of Jesus". No, Messenger Muhammad's message does not contain the familiar diatribes of those that pontificate and "jaw-jack" about the most serious issues of our time.

Muhammad's message is strong medicine. And the articles found in this collection will no doubt be dubbed offensive to sensitive readers whose appetite for information has been formed from exposure to Cable TV news programs the likes of which are looped repeatedly on a 24-hour rotation via CNN and FOX news. The "talking heads" who are put before the public to discuss the problems facing America have been approved of by the same sources who have created the problems. So, it is no wonder that they offer no solutions to the serious political, economic and moral problems of Amrica; the real solutions remain hidden while the problems are, in fact, intensifying.

The Most Honorable Elijah Muhammad and what we affectionately refer to as His "life-giving teachings" have established a model inside of a bleak and woeful time in America. His teachings established for the Black community a nation inside a nation. His teachings are the source of Malcolm X's ideology and world-view. His teachings are responsible for Muhammad Ali's history as an "athlete-activist" and Messenger Muhammad's desire that Black people in America give up the names of our former slave masters is what resulted in Cassius Clay becoming the internationally recognized Muhammad Ali. Messenger Muhammad's teachings produced numerous highly acclaimed students of his that all positively impacted the Black community and the American general public in major ways.

His teachings need to be explored and studied with the motivation for implementing the principles that he articulates to bring about on a mass scale, the solutions that they have produced on the small scale. We invite you to join us in this important work

NOTE: The Most Honorable Elijah Muhammad's writings and teachings in his role as "Messenger" Muhammad date from 1935-1975. From an exalted position He has continued to speak by guiding and instructing His best student-the Honorable Minister Louis Farrakhan from 1975 to the present. So, for a full assessment of the message of the Most Honorable Elijah Muhammad one must include both periods. **He Lives!**

-Demetric Muhammad, September 2018

An Invincible Truth Volume II

Dedication ii

Introduction: Strong Medicine iii

August 3, 1957 - The Islamic World 17
    Most Beautiful 17
    Negro "Dumbest" 18
    Making History 19

August 10, 1957 - The Islamic World 21
    History Makers 22

August 17, 1957 - The Islamic World 25
    No Equal 25
    98% Dissatisfied 26
    Steel 27

August 24, 1957 - The Islamic World 29

August 31, 1957 - The Islamic World 32
    The Making of a Race of Devils 32

September 7, 1957 - The Islamic World 35

September 21, 1957 - The Islamic World 38
    Devil's Exile, Moses is Sent 38

September 28, 1957 - The Islamic World 40
    Like Animals 40
    Tricked by Moses 42

October 5, 1957 - The Islamic World 43
    The Devils Go Back to the Holy Land to Conquer 43

October 12, 1957 - The Islamic World 46
    Whites' Secret 46

October 19, 1957 - The Islamic World 50
    Setback 50

"Smooth Lies"	51
October 26, 1957 - The Islamic World	53
Run Down	54
November 2, 1957 - The Islamic World	56
One God	56
God's Rivals	57
Why Not Obey	57
Devil's Way	58
November 9, 1957 - The Islamic World	59
Unity is Key	59
Know Self	60
End to Dependence	60
One Meal Daily	61
November 16, 1957 - The Islamic World	62
Gods Didn't Exist	62
Not Invented	63
Life Changed	64
Natural Religion	65
November 30, 1957 - The Islamic World	66
Islam Typical	67
No Sickness	67
Now is Time	68
December 7, 1957 - The Islamic World	70
Unable to See	70
Devils	71
December 14, 1957 - The Islamic World	72
The Destruction of Integration	72

Against Nature	72
Destroyed Slaves	73
As It's Written	73
December 21, 1957 - The Islamic World	**75**
Prophets Listed	75
Five Principles	76
Christ No Christian	77
December 28, 1957 - The Islamic World	**78**
Feared by Whites	79
Preparing Place	79
January 4, 1958 – The Islamic World	**81**
From God	82
Salvation	82
January 11, 1958 – The Islamic World	**85**
Only Peace	85
Discounts Calendar	86
January 18, 1958 - The Islamic World	**88**
No Son Mentioned	88
Prisoner-Converts	89
Cites Bible "Errors"	89
January 25, 1958 - The Islamic World	**91**
Jesus Not Alive	91
Divine Family	92
February 1, 1958 - The Islamic World	**94**
Cites Verses	94
Great Deceivers	95
Knows Enemies	95

February 8, 1958; – The Islamic World 97
   Recognize Truth 97
   Try To Convince You 98
February 15, 1958 - The Islamic World 100
   Devils for Friends 100
   Some Questions 101
March 1, 1958 - The Islamic World 103
   Prayer In Islam 103
      To Allah 103
      Purifies Heart 104
      Scholarly Work 104
March 8, 1958 - The Islamic World 106
   False Charges Made Against Prophets 106
      Guilty Party 107
      Makes Mockery 107
      Look at Success 107
March 15, 1958 - The Islamic World 109
   The Bible's Wicked and Filthy Charges Against the Righteous. 109
      Poison 109
      Charges 110
April 12, 1958 - The Islamic World 112
      Mistakes 112
      LOST MEMBERS 113
April 26, 1958 - The Islamic World 115
      Mischief-Making 115
June 28, 1958 - The Islamic World 117
      Clear Language 118
July 5, 1958 - The Islamic World 119

July 26, 1958 - The Islamic World 121
    Love Meddling 122
August 2, 1958 - The Islamic World 123
    WE MUST HAVE SOME EARTH 123
        Satisfied With Nothing 123
        Permanent Home 124
Rare Articles Section 126
A NATION IN A NATION 127
A UNITED BLACK NATION 130
A UNITED BLACK NATION II 132
ALLAH SAYS: ACCEPT YOUR OWN 135
    Lost and Found People 135
    Made To Serve Enemy 135
    Height of Ignorance 136
ALLAH COMES FROM HEAVEN INTO HELL 137
    Allah Comes From Heaven Into Hell 137
    Lost and Found Nation of Islam 138
ALLAH OFFERS YOU A FUTURE 139
AMERICA PERSECUTES THE MUSLIMS 141
AMERICANS PERSECUTE THE MUSLIMS, WHAT WILL BE HER END? ...145
AMERICA WILL DESTROY HERSELF 148
    INTERPRETATION 148
    Satan Exalts Himself 148
    Had Army of Elephants 149
    Took 20 Years 149
AMERICA'S DOOM 151
    Must Reap What Is Sown 151
    Not Learned Love of Self 151

Jehovah's Wonderful Story 152

Sign of the Judgment 153

AN EVIL AND INDECENT RACE (WHITES) 155

Real Devils are Enemies. 155

Filthy, Wicked Show 156

BATTLE IN THE SKY IS NEAR 158

CORRUPTION 161

DECEIVED 164

DOOM OF AMERICA 166

FREE SLAVE? —FREE MASTER? 169

GET KNOWLEDGE TO BENEFIT SELF 173

"HAVE WE QUALIFIED MEN AND WOMEN FOR SELF-GOVERNMENT?" 177

Plenty of Scholars, Scientists 177

We Have No Future 178

List of Murders 178

"HAVE WE QUALIFIED MEN AND WOMEN FOR SELF-GOVERNMENT?" II 180

Want to "Socialize" 180

Afraid to Disobey 181

Watch Your "Friends" 181

HELP SELF BEFORE HELPING OTHERS 183

HELP SELF BEFORE HELPING OTHERS II 186

THE HOPEFUL AND THE HOPELESS 188

KNOW THYSELF 190

KNOW THYSELF II 192

No Justice for So-Called Negroes 194

NO JUSTICE FOR US IN USA 196

INJUSTICE INCREASED 196

HITS FREE DEVIL MURDERS 197

DELIVER POOR AND NEEDY	197
PEACE?	199
PEACE? II	201
ROBBED AND SPOILED	203
SEPARATION	205
SEPARATION IS A MUST	207
SEPARATION OR DEATH	209
SEPARATION OR DEATH II	211
SEPARATION OR DEATH III	213
SEPARATION OR DEATH IV	215
SEPARATION OR TROUBLE?	217
SEPARATION SOLVES THE PROBLEM	220
SOME OF THIS EARTH	222
SOME OF THIS GOOD EARTH THAT WE CAN CALL OUR OWN	224
THE BLINDNESS OF NEGRO PREACHERS	226
THE COMING OF THE SON OF MAN	229
THE DOOM	231
THE DOOM DRAWS NEAR	233
THE END	235
Prey to Government	235
Something of Past	235
Allah Against Whites	236
Sins are Greatest	236
THE GREAT DECEIVER	238
THE GREAT DECEIVERS	238
Failed to Consult Messenger	238
Words of Deception	239
Let Us Enjoy Freedom	239

In For Great Surprise	240
THE SO-CALLED NEGRO LEADERSHIP	242
THE SO-CALLED NEGRO LEADERSHIP II	245
THE SO-CALLED NEGRO LEADERSHIP III	247
THE TRUTH	249
Families to Themselves	249
How Independence Is Born	250
Intelligent Will Agree	250
It's God In Islam	250
TRUTH, Part II	252
Author of the Truth	252
The Light of Truth	252
Our Unity Demanded	253
Whites Made Mischief	253
TRUTH, Part III	255
THE TRUTH IV	257
20 Million In U.S.	257
Angry At Each Other	257
Paid For Our Home	258
THE TRUTH V	260
Submit to Allah	260
Murderers By Nature	260
The Time	260
Negro Progress Slow	261
THE TRUTH VI	262
"Islam"	262
Moslem Shriners	262
Islam Free	262

THE TRUTH VII 263
    He Had to Wait 263
    Negroes Reared by Foes 263
    Tribe of Shabazz 264
    Truth Shall Make You Free 265
UNITY 266
WE MUST BE OURSELVES 268
WE MUST HAVE LAND AS OTHER NATIONS 270
We Must Have More Than A Job 273
What Is Un-American? 275
What the So-Called Negro Must Do 279
Index 282
Gratitude 284

AUGUST 3, 1957 - THE ISLAMIC WORLD

New York Amsterdam News

Whatever is in the Heavens and whatever is in the Earth submits to the God of black mankind – the Sun, the Moon, the Stars, and the powers that uphold them are from the original nation (Black Mankind). He is the First and the Last.

The black man produces these four colors, brown, red, yellow and white. The original people, whom the white race found here (Red people), were the brothers of the Black Man. They are referred to as Red Indians.

The Indian part of the name must refer to the name of the country from which they came, India. The All Wise Allah said that they came here sixteen thousand years ago, and they were exiled from India for breaking the law of Islam.

All of our colors, brown, red and yellow, have ruled since the black. The white race, the most recent made color, ruled all the other colors for the past six thousand years. Much will be said about this later color further on.

Why is the Black Man just coming into his own? Because he desired to try getting experience (or trying everything) of himself. Today you see every color in power but the black man, yet he is the originator of all. Now the Great Mahdi (God in person) with His infinite wisdom, knowledge and understanding, is going to put the original black man as he was at first, the God and Ruler of the Universe.

MOST BEAUTIFUL

Notice the general awakening of this No. 1 man of this people throughout the World of Mankind, the crushed ones of the five above-mentioned colors. That last six thousand years has witnessed the most terrible blows to the complete destruction of this color.

Their color is most adapted to any part of our Planet under any climatic condition. The color of their eyes (black and white) is of all others, the best – the most beautiful of all. Their black hair, white teeth are all the best for they are the best people.

They haven't had their day in many thousands of years. Fifty thousand years ago, according to the Word of Allah, he had his fall and six thousand years ago he had his complete fall. (I shouldn't use the word fall, for it was not. He only allowed the weaker of Himself to Rule.)

When he put the last color of his color into his power, the white color or race, they became the real enemy of the father (Black Man) and tried and are still trying to exterminate the original color (Black) by many ways and means.

Today, the White Race, the black's worst enemies, has planned to make a last try of destroying the black man by pretending to be their friends and allow intermarriage.

Many Americans (especially the Southerners) don't like the idea, but will finally be persuaded by their more learned men when they see no other way of making a final stroke at the Black Man. It will be short-lived for the Judgment will sit, and the agreement will be broken between the Blacks and Whites (the So-Called Negroes) as it is written (Isaiah 29:17,18)

NEGRO "DUMBEST"

The original man (Black) has been without the knowledge of himself for a long time and this one (the American So-Called Negroes), of all his kind, is the dumbest to the knowledge of self, due to the way his slave master teaches and trains him.

But this is the time of the awakening of this poor slave and no powers on earth or in the Heavens above will be able to prevent it.

For it is the will and work of Allah (God) and His choice of the people.

He has chosen the so-called negroes, but they being blinded and made deaf and dumb, have not but a few, chosen Allah to be their God; but they will after they see more of His power displayed in the west and they will see it. It's going on now. It is a must with Allah to restore the lost sheep.

The Black people are by nature the righteous. They have love and mercy in their hearts even after trying to live the life of the devils – this is still recognized in them. When they are fully in the knowledge of self, they will do righteousness and live in peace among themselves.

One can't judge them now for they are not their own selves. We, the original nation of the earth, says Allah, the Maker of everything – Sun, Moon and Stars and the race called white race, are the writers of the Bible and Qu-ran.

MAKING HISTORY

We make such history once every twenty-five thousand years. When such history is written, it is done by twenty-four of our scientists.

One acts as Judge or God for the others and twenty-three actually do the work of getting up the future of the Nation, and all is put into One Book and at intervals where such and such part or portion will come to pass, that people will be given that part of the book through one among that people from one of the Twelve (12 Major Scientists) as it is then called a Scripture which actually means a script of writing from something original or book.

There is a significance to the number 24 Scientists and the 25,000 years. The number twenty-four Scientists used is in accordance with the hours in our day and the measurement of our circumference of our Planet around with the Equator and in the region of our Poles, Arctic and Antarctic Oceans.

Our Planet is not exactly 25,000 miles in circumference, it is 24,896 miles and we, according to Astronomy, don't have a full 24-hour day but near that – 23 hours, 56 minutes and 46 seconds. The change made in our Planet's rotation at the Poles is about one minute a year and takes 25,000 years to bring about a complete change in the region of the Poles.

Hurry and lose no time in joining onto your Own Kind. The Time of this World is at hand.

AUGUST 10, 1957 - THE ISLAMIC WORLD

New York Amsterdam News

In the change made in our planet's rotation at the Poles is about one minute a year and takes 25,000 years to bring about a complete change in the region of the Poles. The actual Poles are inclined 23 1/2 degrees to the plane of its orbit. The original black nation used 23 scientists to write the future of that nation for the next 25,000 years, and the 24th is the Judge or the one God, Allah. Allah taught me that, once upon a time they made history to last for 35,000 years. Let me stop here and say this:

My people must know the truth, the God's truth; the time is at hand! They are reared and taught by the devils and they know it not; and being ignorant of the truth, they offer opposition to the God of their salvation, Who is the very author of Truth.

I am His Messenger. They do this because of the fear of the devils. They are made to believe that without the friendship of the devils they would perish.

The (Bible) warns them against the friendship of the devils (James 4:4) "Whosoever, therefore will be a friend of the World in the enemy of God" The sixth verse of the same chapter reads: "Submit yourselves therefore to God. Resist the devil and he will flee from you."

Do they dare resist the devils? No! Being without the Truth of Allah and the devil, they are afraid and that fear is the cause of their suffering and will be the cause of their destruction in Hell with the devils whom they love and fear.

Preachers, who read and study to teach the Bible to your own people, get the understanding of it first before teaching it to the blind, deaf and dumb of your own people lest you lead both them and your own selves to Hell. Remember – your white slave masters are your translators and teachers of the Bible.

They – who will not give you Justice under this law – will not give you Truth and Justice in the Word of God! Stop being a fool for the false friendships of the devils. Stop teaching your people to love your enemies. Which is a lie that the devils teach and claim that Jesus taught it. God doesn't give laws which are contrary to our nature to do them.

HISTORY MAKERS

We are the makers of divine histories and who is better in knowledge than Allah (God)?

Man is easily made, but the sun, moon and stars are much harder to make. Yet we are the makers of them. In making the moon, it was not our original father's intention to make the moon as it is). His real intention was to destroy the moon (Earth) but failed, and all others who make such attempts will fail.

What! Do you disbelieve it? Do you not see that the devils are trying to make them a Satellite to make you believe that they are the Masters of the Heavens and Earth, as it is written of them in the Bible and Holy Qur'an. (Isaiah 14:13-16th verses)

They destroyed other people, cities and opened not the house of his prisoners. None has fulfilled this prophecy better than America. She has destroyed other nation's cities while she has not suffered the loss of one of her cities by a foreign Nation, while preaching the Freedom of her own people from the Powers of other Nations.

She holds a whole nation (the So-Called Negroes) prisoner, and refuses to open the door of freedom, justice and equality to them. She threatens to go to War against other Nations who hold any of her citizens prisoners. They now boast of building rockets to land on our Moon (of which it can't and won't be done): and to build a small contraption to try circling the Earth like our Moon, which we have made to revolve around the Earth.

The following is from the Holy Qur'an: "And we (the devils) sought to reach heaven but we found it filled with strong guards and flames: and we (the devils) used to sit in some of the sitting places thereof to steal a hearing. But he who tries to listen now finds a flame lying in wait for him." (Holy Qur'an 72:8,9)

The devils are universal snoopers. They pretend to be interested in your spiritual meetings, but only to listen to what you are saying among yourselves. They even pretend to want to accept Islam, only to sit among the Muslims to steal all they have to say among themselves.

You may see him in all of the churches and gathering places of the So-Called Negroes to listen in on their meetings, to keep them from accepting the Truth. (Islam) The So-Called Negroes think that it is an honor to have the devils come among them, because they are ignorant to this, their open enemies' intentions.

I am for the separation of my people from their enemies: that they share not in the enemies' destruction, even though I may lose my own life in this daring attempt to save them by the plain, simple truth of God and power. It must be done and will be done regardless of whom or what. It can be done in one day, but Allah desires to make Himself known in the West, as it is written of Him.

Our sixty-six trillion years from the Moon has proven a great and wise show of the original power, to build wonders in the Heavens and Earth. Six thousand years ago, or to be more exact 6,600 years ago, as Allah taught me, our Nation gave birth to another God whose name was Yakub. He started studying the life germ of man to try making it a new creation (new man) whom our 24 Scientists had foretold 8,400 years before the birth of Mr. Yakub, and the Scientists were aware of his birth and work before he was born, as they are today of the intentions or ideas of the present World.

Hurry and lose not time in joining onto your Own Kind. The Time of this World is at hand.

AUGUST 17, 1957 - THE ISLAMIC WORLD

New York Amsterdam News

The knowledge of Mr. Yakub's birth, work and death was known eight thousand four hundred years before he was born. This scientist is known to be the God of this World, (the Father of the Caucasian Race) known in certain places, in the Bible, as being the Father of the Tribes – and, is called in the English Language, Jacob. Jesus mentioned him as being the Father of Sin, the devil (John 8:41, 44) of which he is right.

According to the word of Allah (God), to me. Mr. Yakub was seen by the 23 Scientists of the black nation, fifteen thousand years ago. To be exact, fifteen thousand forty-three years ago. They predicted that in the year 8,400 (that was in our calendar year before this world of the white race), this man (Yakub) would be born twenty miles from the present Holy City, Mecca, Arabia.

And, that at the time of his birth, the satisfaction and dissatisfaction of the people would be: 70% satisfied, 30% dissatisfied.

And, that when this man (Mr. Yakub) is born, he will change the civilization (the World), and produce a new race of people, who would rule the Original Black Nation for six thousand years (from the nine thousandth year to the fifteen thousandth year).

After that time, the original black nation would give birth to one, whose wisdom, knowledge and power would be infinite. One who the World would recognize as being the greatest and mightiest God, since the creation of the universe. And, that He would destroy Yakub's world and restore the original nation or ancient nation, into power to rule forever.

NO EQUAL

This mighty one, is known under many names. He has no

equal. There never was one like Him. He is referred to in the Bible as God, Almighty, and in some places as Jehovah, the God of Gods, and the Lord of lords.

The Holy Qur'an refers to Him as Allah, the One God: besides Him, there is no God and there is none like Him: the Supreme Being: the mighty, the wise, the best knower; the light; the life giver; the Mahdi (this is He, whom I have met and am missioned by).

He, also, is referred to as the Christ, the second Jesus. The Son of Man, who is wise and is all powerful. He knows how to reproduce the Universe; and, the people of His choice. He will remove and destroy the present, old warring wicked World of Yakub (the Caucasian World) and set up a World of Peace and Righteousness, out of the present so-called negroes, who are rejected and despised by this World. (Fly to Him, so-called negroes; he is your first and last friend).

98% DISSATISFIED

Mr. Yakub, was, naturally, born out of the 30% dissatisfied. As we know, wherever there is a longing or demand for a change, nature will produce that man, who will bring it about.

Allah (God) taught me, that the present percentage of dissatisfaction is 98%, near 100%, with the present ruling powers.

This 100% dissatisfied, will bring about a 100% change. Yakub did not bring about a 100% change, but near, (90%). Allah (God), to Whom praises are due, said: "That when Yakub was six years old, one day, he was sitting down playing with two pieces of steel.

He noticed the magnetic power in the steel attracting the other. He looked up at his Uncle and said: "Uncle, when I get to be an old man, I am going to make a people who shall rule you." The Uncle said: "What will you make: something to make mischief and cause bloodshed in the land?" Yakub said:

"Nevertheless, Uncle, I know that which you do not know."

And it was at that moment, the boy Yakub, first came into the knowledge of just who he was – born to make trouble, break peace, kill and destroy his own people with a made enemy to the Black Nation.

STEEL

He learned his future from playing with steel. It is steel and more steel, that his made race (the white race), are still playing with. Steel has become the most useful of all metal for the people. What he really saw in playing with the two pieces of steel, was the magnetic Power of Attraction.

The one, attracting and drawing the other under its Power. In this, he saw an unlike human being, made to attract others, who could, with the knowledge of tricks and lies, rule the Original Black Man: - until that Nation could produce one greater and capable of overcoming and making manifest his race of tricks and lies, with a Nation of Truth, and alike.

Yakub was the founder of unalike attract and alike repels, though Mr. Yakub was a member of the Black Nation. He began school at the age of four. He had an unusual size head. When he had grown up, the others referred to him as the "big head scientist."

At the age of 18, he had finished all of the colleges and universities of his nation and was seen preaching on the streets of Mecca, making converts. He made such impressions on the people that many began following him.

He learned, from studying the germ of the black man, under the microscope, that there were two people in him, and that one was black, the other brown.

He said, if he could successfully, separate the one from the other, he could graft the brown germ into its last stage, which would be white. With his wisdom, he could make the white, which he discovered was the weaker of the black germ – which would be unalike, rule the Black Nation for a time (until a greater one than Yakub was born).

    This new idea put him to work finding the necessary converts to begin grafting his new race of people. He began by teaching Islam, with promises of luxury to those who would believe and follow him.

Hurry and Join onto your own kind. The Time of this World is at hand.

AUGUST 24, 1957 - THE ISLAMIC WORLD

New York Amsterdam News
(Continued from previous article)

As Mr. Yakub continued to preach for converts, he told his people he would make the others work for them. (This promise came to pass). Naturally, there are always some people around who would like to have others do their work. Those are the ones who fell for Mr. Yakub's teaching, one hundred percent.

As he made converts in and around the Holy City Mecca, persecutions set in. The Authorities became afraid of such powerful teachings, with promises of luxury and making slaves of others. As they began making arrests of those who believed the teaching, the officers would go back and find, to their surprise, others still teaching and believing it.

Finally, they arrested Mr. Yakub. But, it only increased the teachings. They kept persecuting and arresting Yakub's followers until they filled all the jails.

The officers finally reported to the King, that there was no room to put a prisoner in – if arrested. "All the jails are filled; and, when we go out into the streets, we find them still teaching. What shall we do with them?" The King questioned the officers on just what the teachings were; and, of the name of the Leader.

The officers gave the King the answers to everything. The King said: "This is not the name of that man." (Yakub was going in an assumed name). The King said: "Take me to this man." On entering the prison, the King was shown Yakub's cell.

The King said: "As-Salaam-Alaikum, Mr. Yakub." Yakub said: Wa-Alaikum-Salaam." The King said: "So you are Mr. Yakub?" He said: "Yes, I am." The King said: "Yakub, I have come to see if we could work out some agreement that would bring about an end to this trouble. What would you suggest?"

Mr. Yakub told the King: "If you give me and my followers

everything to start civilization as you have and furnish us with money and other necessities of life (general care) for twenty years, I will take my followers and we will go from you."

The King was pleased with the suggestion or condition made by Yakub, and agreed to take care of them for twenty years, until Yakub's followers were able to go for themselves.

After learning who Mr. Yakub was, they all were afraid of him, and, were glad to make almost any agreement with him and his followers.

The History or future of Mr. Yakub and his people was in the Nation's Book, by the writers (23 Scientists) of our History, 8400 years before his birth. So, the Government began to make preparation for the exiling of Mr. Yakub and his followers. The King ordered everyone rounded up, who was a believer in Mr. Yakub. They took them to the seaport and loaded them on ships.

After rounding them all up into ships, they numbered fifty-nine thousand, nine hundred and ninety-nine people. Yakub made sixty thousand. Their ships sailed out to an Isle in the Aegean Sea called "Pelan" (Bible—Patmos). After they were loaded into the ships, Mr. Yakub examined each of them to see if they were 100% with him: and, to see if they were all healthy and productive people. If not, he would throw them off. Some were found to be unfit and overboard they went.

When they arrived at the Isle, Mr. Yakub said to them: "See how they (the Holy People) have cast us out. Now – if you will choose me to be your King, I will teach you how to go back and rule them all."

Of course, they had already chosen Yakub to be their King at the very start. So, Yakub chose Doctors, Ministers Nurses, and a Cremator for his top laborers. He called these laborers together and told them his plan for making a new people, who would rule for six thousand years.

He called the Doctor first and said: "Doctor, let all the people come to you who want to marry; and, if there comes to you, two real black ones, take a needle and get a little of their blood and go into your room and pretend to be examining it, to see whether their blood would mix.

Then, come and tell them that they will have to find another mate, because their blood does not mix. It was the aim of Yakub to get rid of the Black, and he did. Give them a certificate to take to the Minister, warning the Minister against marrying the couple because their blood does not mix. When there comes to you, two browner ones, take a pretended blood test of them; but, give them a certificate saying that they are eligible to be married.

Hurry and lose not time in joining onto your own kind. The Time of this World is at hand.

AUGUST 31, 1957 - THE ISLAMIC WORLD

The Making of a Race of Devils
New York Amsterdam News

Mr. Yakub's charge to his laborers was very strict – death if one disobeyed. They didn't know what Yakub had in mind until they were given their labor to do. **Notice**: In last weeks' article, he made his laborers, from the chief to the least, liars. The doctor lied about the blood of the two black people who wanted to marry, that it did not mix.

The brown and black could not be married (brown only). The doctors of today hold the same position over people. You go to them to get a blood test to see if you are fit to be married.

Today, they say it is done to see if there are any contagious germs in the blood. I wish that they would enforce such a law today (keep the white from mixing with black – just the opposite). Perhaps we could remain black and not be disgraced by a mixture of all colors.

In the days of Yakub's grafting of the present white race, a new and unalike race among the black nation for six hundred years, his law was – that they should not allow the black to mix with their blood.

His aim was to kill and destroy the black nation. He ordered the nurses to kill all black babies that came to birth among his people, by pricking the brains with a sharp needle as soon as the black child's head is out of his mother.

If the mother is alert (watching the nurse), then the nurse would lie and fool the mother to get possession of her child to murder it, by saying that she (mother) gave birth to an "angel child." And, that she (the nurse) would like to take the baby to Heaven, so when the mother dies, she would have a room with her child in Heaven, for her baby was an angel.

This is the beginning of the first lie or liar; and, it was so that the nurse would take the black baby away on this falsehood and claim that they were taking the poor black baby to Heaven. As Yakub had taught them, they would feed it to wild beasts and if they did not find a wild beast to feed the black babies to, Yakub told the Nurses to give it to the cremator to burn.

Mr. Yakub warned the laborers from the doctor down to this cremator, that if anyone of them failed to carry out his orders, off go their heads.

When there was a birth of a brown baby, the nurse would come and make much ado over it; and would tell the mother that she had given birth to a holy child and that she would nurse it for the next six weeks for her child was going to be a great man (that is when it was a boy baby).

After the first two hundred years, Mr. Yakub had done away with the black babies and all were brown. After another 200 years, he had all yellow or red, which was four hundred years after being on "Pelan." Another 200 years, which brings us to the 600th year, Mr. Yakub had an all pale white race of people on this Isle.

Of course, Mr. Yakub did not live but 150 years; but, his idea continued into practice. He gave his people guidance in the form of literature. What they should do and how to do it (how to rule the black nation.) He said to them: "When you become unalike, (white) you may return to the Holy Land and people, from whom you were exiled."

The Yakub made devils were really pale white, with real blue eyes: which we think are the most ugliest of colors for a human eye. They were called Caucasian – which means, stale faced and weak boned. Later called "Shaitan," which means, according to some of the Arab scholars, "One whose evil effect is not confined to one's self alone but affects others."

There was no good taught to them while on the Island. By teaching the nurses to kill the black baby and save the brown baby; so as to graft the white out of it, by lying to the black mother of the baby, this lie was born into the very nature of the white baby; and, murder for the black people was also born in them – or made by nature a liar and a murderer.

The Black Nation is only fooling themselves to take the Caucasian race otherwise. This is what Jesus learned of their history, before he gave up his work of trying to convert the Jews or white race to the religion of Islam.

And, the same knowledge of them was given to Muhammad by the Imams (or scientists) of Mecca. That is why the war of the Muslims against them came to a stop.

Muhammad was told that he could not reform the devils and that the race had 1,400 more years to live; and, the only way to make righteous people (Muslims) out of them was to graft them back into the black nation.

This grieved Muhammad so much that it caused him heart trouble until his death (age 62 ½ years.) The old scientists used to laugh at Muhammad for thinking he could convert them (the devils) to Islam. This hurt his heart.

Hurry and lose not time in joining onto your own kind. The Time of this World is at hand.

SEPTEMBER 7, 1957 - THE ISLAMIC WORLD

New York Amsterdam News

There are many millions of people on the earth today who are learning, for their first time through my articles, the Truth that Allah has revealed to me, in the person of Master Fard Muhammad, to whom be praised in the Heavens and the Earth forever (He, of whom not one in a thousand know as God in person).

Last week's article told you how the White Race was grafted out of the black nation: - by way of murdering the black baby and saving the brown; and, marrying the brown onto the brown, by keeping up the practice of the birth control law – until the brown was grafted into its last stage – which is white.

This made the white race murderers, liars and universal deceivers. They are wicked by nature and can't be trusted as a friend, by the black people; only to your sorrow.

They can't do anything about how they were made; nor can you and I do anything about it unless we graft them back into our own nation; so, said Allah to me. After we have been taught the knowledge of them, we should shun them.

We should protect ourselves and our children, from becoming a victim of their evils; and, being deceived by them; taking them for the beloved people of God and God's Ministers of Truth; or be carried away in love for them because of their attraction (unlikeness and great wealth and richness), which Allah has given to them to try you. Nor, should you allow them to deceive you today with their false love making, love songs, soft voices, and the false Civil Rights Law.

All this is being done to deceive you and cause you to suffer Hell fire with them. They know that you have an unlimited future if you join onto your own kind, and accept Allah and the True Religion, Islam. They really know that their race has– "no future;" and, will be wiped from the face of the Earth by Allah, as if they had not been. I am warning you. Take Heed To It, Or Leave it!

They were not created to be saved. They don't lead you to anything but evil and indecencies. Fear them not! You are the righteous, the powerful; and, you shall rule after them. Thanks to our God, Who has come to save us, and teaches us the Wisdom – that which we did not know – in the person of Master Fard Muhammad.

After their grafting from black to white, they were called Caucasian, which means: "one who is weak boned, and stale faced, wicked by nature." These are the real devils.

Mr. Yakub taught his made devils on Pelan: "That when you go back to the Holy Black Nation, rent a room in their homes. Teach your wives to go out the next morning around the neighbors of the people, and tell them that you heard her talking about them last night.

When you have gotten them fighting and killing each other, then ask them to let you help settle their disputes, and restore peace among them. If they agree, then you will be able to rule them both." This method the white race practices on the black nation, the world over. They upset their peace, by putting one against the other, and then rule them after dividing them.

This is the reason why the American so-called Negroes can never agree on unity among themselves, which would put them on top overnight. The devils keep them divided by paid informers (stool pigeons) from among themselves. They keep such fools among us. But, the real truth of the devils sometimes converts the informers and brings them over to us as true believers. We don't bother about killing them, as I am not teaching that which I want to be kept as a secret; but, that which the World has not known and should know.

After Yakub's made devils were among the Holy People of

Islam (the Black Nation), for six months, they had our people at war with each other. The Holy People were unable to understand, just why they could not get along in peace with each other, until they took the matter to the King.

The King told the Holy People of the black nation, that the trouble they were having was caused by the white devils in their midst. And, that there would be no peace among them until they drove these white made devils from among them.

The Holy people prepared to drive the devils out from among them. The King said: "Gather every one of the devils up and strip them of our costume. Put an apron on them to hide their nakedness. Take all the literature from them and take them by way of the desert. Send a caravan armed with rifles, to keep the devils going Westward. Don't allow one of them to turn back: and, if they are lucky to get across the Arabian Desert, let them go into the hills of West Asia (as they now call the place Europe).

Write me and join onto your own kind. The time of this World is at hand.

SEPTEMBER 21, 1957 - THE ISLAMIC WORLD

Devil's Exile, Moses is Sent
New York Amsterdam News

Yakub's made devils were driven out of Paradise, into the Hills of West Asia (Europe) and stripped of everything but the language. They walked across the hot, sandy desert, into the land where long years of both trouble and joy awaited them; but, they finally made it. (Not all: many died in the desert).

Once there, they were roped in, to keep them out of Paradise. To make sure, the Muslims, who lived along the borders of East and West Asia, were ordered to patrol the border to keep Yakub's devils into West Asia (now called Europe); so that the original nation (Black man) could live in peace; and, that the devils could be alone to themselves, to do as they pleased, as long as they didn't try crossing the East border.

The soldiers patrolled the border armed with swords, to prevent the devils from crossing. This went on for two thousand years. After that time, Musa (Moses) was born; the man whom Allah would send to these exiled devils, to bring them again into the light of civilization. Before we take up this first two thousand years of the devils, being exiled on our Planet, let us not lose sight of what, and how they were made; and, the God who made them, Mr. Yakub.

Since we have learned that Mr. Yakub was an original man (Black), the ignorant of our people may say, that: "If Yakub was a Black man and the father of the Devils, then he was a devil." That is like one saying, "The horse is as much a mule as the mule."

Or, that "an orange or lemon is a much grapefruit as the grapefruit:" – because the grapefruit is grafted from the orange and lemon. They are not alike because the grafted is no more original.

Just what have we learned, or rather are learning from this Divine revelation, of our enemies, the devils? Answer: We are learning that Truth, which has been kept a secret for six thousand years, concerning the white race, who have deceived us. We learn what is meant of the Bible's symbolic teachings: that, they were made from dust.

This only tends to convey the idea that they were created from nothing: which means the low and humble origin of such creation.

Again, we learn who the Bible (Genesis 1:26) is referring to in the saying: "Let us make man." This "US" was fifty-nine thousand nine hundred and ninety-nine (59, 999) Black men and women making or grafting them into the likeness or image of the original man.

Not that they are the same but have the ways of a human being: as they are referred to as "Mankind," – not the real original man, but a being made like the original being in the sense of human beings.

The Holy Qur'an throws a great light on the Truth of the creation of this pale, white race of devils "O mankind, surely we have created you from a male and a female" (Chapter 49:13). This makes it very easy to understand who it is referring to. "What mankind?" "Surely, we created man from sperm mixed (with ovum) to try him, so we have made him hearing and seeing." (Chapter 76:2)

Inasmuch as these Chapters have a spiritual reference to the Spiritual Creation of the Last Messenger, it is equally true that they refer to the physical creation of the white race. In another place, the Holy Quran says, "We have created man and now he is an open disputer."

SEPTEMBER 28, 1957 - THE ISLAMIC WORLD

New York Amsterdam News
(Continued from Previous Article)

Yakub's race of devils were exiled in the hills and caves of West Asia (as they now call it Europe). They were without anything to start civilization and became savages. They remained in such condition for two thousand years – no guide or literature.

They lost all knowledge of civilization. The Lord, God of Islam, taught me that some of them tried to graft themselves back into the black nation, but they had nothing to go by. A few were lucky enough to make a start; and got as far as what you call the gorilla. In fact, all of the monkey family is from this two-thousand-year history of the white race in Europe.

Being deprived of Divine guidance for their disobedience; the making of mischief and causing bloodshed in the Holy Nation of the original black people by lies, they became so savage that they lost all their sense of shame.

They stared going nude as they are doing today (and leading the so-called Negroes into the very acts).

In those days, they made their homes in the caves on the hill-sides. There is a whole chapter devoted to them in the Holy Qur'an. They had it very hard, trying to save themselves from being destroyed by wild beasts, that were plentiful at that time in Europe.

LIKE ANIMALS

Being without a guide, they started walking on their hands and feet like all the animals; and learned to climb trees as good as any of the animals. At night, they would climb up into trees, carrying large stones and clubs to fight the wild beasts that would come prowling around at night, to keep them from eating their families.

Their next and best weapons were the dogs. They tamed some of these dogs to live in the caves with their families, to help protect them from the wild beasts. After a time, the dogs held a high place among the family because of his fearlessness to attack the enemies of his master. Today, the dog is still loved by the white race and is given more justice than the so-called Negroes and is called the white man's best friend. This comes from the cave days.

After two thousand years of living as a savage, Allah raised up Musa (Moses) to bring the white race again into civilization: to take their place as rulers as Yakub had intended for them. Musa (Moses) became their God and Leader. He brought them out of the caves; taught them to believe in Allah; taught them to wear clothes; how to cook their food; how to season it with salt; what beef they should kill and eat, and the ones they shouldn't eat; and, how to use fire for their service. Moses taught them against putting the female cow under burden.

He established for them, Friday as the day to eat fish, and not to eat meat (beef) on that day. And, fish is the main menu in many of the whites' homes today on Fridays.

They were so evil (savage) that Moses had to build a ring of fire around him at night; and, he would sleep in the center of the ring to keep the devils from harming him. They were afraid of fire and are still afraid of fire.

Allah said, that: "One day, Moses told them he was going to have fish come up from the sea that night so that tomorrow we will have some fish.

On the next day, the fish were there. Moses had a boatload sent up from Egypt. Moses said: "See! The sea came up last night and brought us some fish." One of the savages was a little smart and he said to Moses: "Where is the water?"

TRICKED BY MOSES

From then on, Moses recognized the fact that he could not say just anything to them. He had a very hard time trying to civilize them. Once they gave Moses so much trouble that he took a few sticks of dynamite, went up on the mountainside, placed them into the ground, and went back to get the ones who were giving the most trouble.

He said to them: "Stand there on the edge of the mountain and you will hear the voice of God." They stood there about 300 in number. Moses set the fuse off and it killed all of them.

The Imams got after Moses for performing this trick on the devils. Moses said to the Imams: "If you only knew how much trouble these devils give me, you would do as I do." Moses taught the devils that if they would follow him and obey him, Allah would give them a place among the Holy People. Most of them believed Moses, just to get out of the caves.

Write me and join onto your own kind.

OCTOBER 5, 1957 - THE ISLAMIC WORLD

The Devils Go Back to the Holy Land to Conquer
New York Amsterdam News
(Continued From Previous Article)

The Imams recognized the tremendous job Musa (Moses) had to try civilizing the savages. These enemies of the righteous Black Nation of Earth, now had to take the place as the Rulers and Conquerors of the Earth. The devils were given the knowledge and power to bring every living thing, regardless of its kind of life, into subjection.

"And God said 'Let us make man in our image, after our likeness; Let them have dominion over the fish of the Sea; and over the fowl of the Air; and over the cattle, and over all of the earth; and over every creeping thing that creepeth upon the earth: And God said unto them: 'Be fruitful, and multiply; and replenish the earth and subdue it." (Gen 1: 26, 28).

The above was all necessary if the devils were to rule as a God of the World. They must conquer, and bring into subjection, all life upon the Earth – not land life alone, but they must subdue the Sea and the life therein—Master everything, until a Greater Master or God comes, which would mean the end of their power over the life of our Earth.

We all bear witness, that the scripture quoted above, refers to the Caucasian Race. They are the only people who answer that description, and work for the past 4,000 years.

They have subdued the people and most every kind of living thing upon the Earth. God has blessed them to exercise all their knowledge and blessed them with guides (Prophets) from among our own people; and with the rain and seasons of the Earth.

Today, their wealth is great upon the Earth. Their sciences

of worldly good have sent them not only after the wealth of other than their own people, but even after the lives and property of their own kind. They have tried to re-people (replenish) the earth with their own kind, by skillfully killing off the Black Man and mixing their blood into the Black Woman.

But, the job is too big for them to ever conquer. The Black Nation, including its other three colors, Brown, Red and Yellow, outnumber the Caucasian Race eleven to one.

"God created them in His image." (Gen. 1:27). They are in the image and likeness of a human being (Black Man) but are altogether a different kind of human being than that of the Black human beings.

Their pale white skin: their blue eyes (even disliked by themselves) tells any Black Man or Woman, that in those blue and green eyes, there just can't be any sincere love and friendship for them. They are unalike, and we are alike. Alike repels – unalike attracts. The very characteristics of Black and White are so very different.

Black people have a heart of good, love and mercy. Such a heart, nature did not give to the White Race. This is where the So-Called Negroes are deceived in this Devil Race. They think they have the same kind of heart: but the White Race know better. They have kept it as a secret among themselves, that they be able to deceive the Black people.

They have been, and still are successful in deceiving the Black Man, under the disguise of being one who wants peace, love and friendship with the World, and with God – at the same time, making war with the World, to destroy peace, love and friendship of the Black Nation.

A brother loves and desires for his brother, what he desires for himself. So-Called Negroes, do you have this kind of love and desire from the White Race for you? Why? Because as I have shown to you, they are not your brothers, by nature. They are fully showing you, this day, openly, that they are different from you; and, you are different from them.

Why not try making brotherly love and friendship with your own kind first? To see you trying to integrate with the very enemy of yours, and God, shows, beyond a shadow of a doubt, that you don't know yourself nor your enemies; or rather are lost in love for our enemies. I know you, who love your enemy, don't like that I tell you this Truth. But, I can't help it – Come What May, God has put upon me this mission, and I must do His Will or burn.

Are you with me to do the Will of God, or the will of the devil and the disbelieving people? I know you are, for you have and are learning more Truth (though you are afraid of it) from my articles than you have ever read or ever will read. Fear Not! Allah is on our side; to give you and me the Kingdom.

There is a second Adam mentioned throughout the History of the first Adam. I will tell you who he is soon, in this column.

Write me and join onto your own kind. The Time of this World is at hand.

OCTOBER 12, 1957 - THE ISLAMIC WORLD

New York Amsterdam News
(Continued from Previous Article)

The greatest thing that ever came to you and me is The Truth; especially when it is in our favor. Of all the knowledge a man may have, the best is the knowledge of self, God and the devil. Without the above knowledge, you are not considered a civilized person: for if we know not our own self, how can we know God and the devil? How can we serve one and eschew the other, without the knowledge of both? Real Truth brings about a change.

The Truth is never wanted by false believers. The people, who have not known the Truth, must be taught it before judging them. If a liar has deceived the people, then Truth will make manifest the liar. Yakub's race of devils were made unalike the original black nation for the purpose of being able to attract the original nation to follow them.

It stands true: white attracts black and black attracts white; but, where the attraction differs is, the black, and especially the so-called Negroes, love the unalike (the white race) while the unalike, by nature, can't love the so-called Negroes.

As you have learned, they were made to hate and kill off the black. They have killed on an average of 100,000,000 for every one thousand years, that they have been on our planet; and, hope to carry 97% of the so-called Negroes here in America to their doom. And, two-thirds of the entire black population of the earth. But, maybe a thorough knowledge of their enemies will reduce this figure.

WHITES' SECRET

The secret of the white race just couldn't be exposed before their time of rule was out. If the original black nation had known that this new, unalike, blue-eyed race would not be accepted by the God of righteousness at the end of six thousand years of their time, there would not have been one left on our planet today.

The knowledge of them was kept as a secret from the common people, as they are symbolically spoken of under the name of "Cain" who murdered his brother.

"God marked Cain so that the people would not recognize the murderer of their righteous brother, lest the people would kill him" (Gen. 4:15): "though God pronounced a curse on Cain, coming from the earth, which had opened her mouth to receive the righteous blood from the murderer's hand.

He was to be from the face of the earth and from the face of God. The earth shall not yield her strength to Cain: and he shall be a fugitive and a vagabond" (Gen. 4:10, 12).

Moses reminded them of this curse in (Deut. 28:45-52). Of course, the so-called Negroes are warned in the same chapter, to let the Divine chastisement or destruction of their enemies serve as a lesson to their future greatness, or they will meet such fate.

The history of our enemies (the Caucasian race) shows that for their creating trouble and causing bloodshed among the righteous, six thousand years ago in Arabia, Allah (God) punished them by driving them out from among the righteous and off the good land of the righteous, onto the worst part of the earth (Europe), for two thousand years.

There, they lost he knowledge of the human family and lived the life of beasts in the untrodden wilderness of our Planet Earth.

God turned merciful to them through the sending of Musa (Moses). After being led by Moses, they began to progress into a very successful race. They changed the caves and hillsides of Europe into beautiful towns and cities.

They built factories making the essential things for their comforts. They suffered many setbacks for their evils against the Prophets of Allah (God) sent among them from time to time. They over-populated Europe, and Allah (God) suffered them to expand further West across the Great Atlantic Ocean, from the following of a half-original man (Christopher Columbus): where they killed the original exiled Indians, whom Allah (God) exiled sixteen thousand years ago from India for their disobediences.

For the last four hundred years, here in the Western Hemisphere, they have dotted the land with thousands of villages, towns, cities, and factories.

They became the most powerful and richest people on earth, only to now lose it along with their lives for their evil doings against we so-called Negroes; and, to avenge the blood of the righteous, whom their fathers killed and mobbed, from the time they started trouble in Paradise, to the persecuting and killing of you and me here today.

The White Race are saying that they should be saved for they have done more for the people than anyone has ever done. What a foolish thing to say. We have been here since the creation of this universe.

Are we so weak, dumb and silly that a baby only six days old has shown or done that which we could not do for ourselves? Our father created worlds and every kind of life and upholds them by His will.

What does the white race have that we didn't give them?

Are they the first to build cities, transportation, ships ploughing the oceans, carrying merchandise and raw materials of all kinds? What have they perfected of all their modern sciences? This is our earth and everything in it, and around it. Can we not make it a Heaven for us as we allowed them and helped them to make one for themselves?

Hurry and lose no time. Join onto your own kind for the Time of this World is at hand.

OCTOBER 19, 1957 - THE ISLAMIC WORLD

New York Amsterdam News
(Continued from Previous Article)

You have learned from the reading of History, that a nation's permanent success depends on its obedience to Allah (God). We have seen the white race (Devils) in Heaven, among the righteous, causing trouble (making mischief and causing bloodshed), until they were discovered (that they were devils).

They made trouble for six months, right in Heaven, deceiving the ancient original people who were Holy. But, when they learned just who was causing the trouble: they, as you have learned in this column, cast the troublemakers out into the worst and poorest part of our Planet Earth.

They were punished by being deprived of Divine Guidance, for two thousand years which brought them almost into the family of wild beasts going upon their all fours; eating raw and unseasoned, uncooked food; living in caves and tree tops, climbing and jumping from one tree to the other.

Even today, they like climbing and jumping. The monkeys are from them. Before their time, there were no such things as monkeys, apes and swine. Read the Holy Qur'an (Chapter 18) entitled "The Cave." The Holy Qur'an mentions them as being turned into apes and swine as a Divine curse, because of their disbelief in Moses.

We do know that both of these animals are loved and befriended by the White Race, along with the dog. But, in all of the Divine curses sent upon the White Race in these days, it is not enough to serve as a warning to that race. They rose up from the caves and hillsides of Europe, went back to Asia: and, have ruled nine-tenths of that great continent.

SETBACK

Muhammad (may the peace and blessings of Allah be upon him) set the devils back for one thousand years. They were released upon the coming of Columbus, and his finding of this western hemisphere. They have been here now over four hundred years. Their worst and unpardonable sins were the bringing of the so-called Negroes here to do their labor.

The Negroes (so-called) have not only given free labor but give their lives on the soil of their master; and, all over the earth wherever his hateful and murdering slave master wants them to go. Now, the slave wants better treatment. They are fast learning today, that these are the children of those who made merchandise out of their fathers. The devil is "the devil" regardless to place and time.

They deceived our fathers and are now deceiving their children, under many false disguises, as though they want to be friends of the black man, such as; integration and inter-marriage.

The devils said to Allah: "I shall certainly come upon them from before them and from behind them; and from their right and from their left; and Thou wilt not find most of them thankful." (Holy Qur'an 7:17). This is being fulfilled in our very eyes today. The devils are doing both.

They come to the so-called Negroes as friends and as open enemies. They go before them, changing the truth into falsehood; and, come behind the Truth-bearer to the Negroes, speaking evil of the Truth. They threaten the Negroes with poverty and imprisonment; and, make rosy promises to them, only to deceive.

They are telling the so-called Negroes that, "they realized that they used to mistreat the Negroes, but know they are going to do better and forget the past. Let us live like brothers for we are all from one God."

"SMOOTH LIES"

Along with such smooth lies, is an offer of one of the devils' women. The poor Negroes fall victim and the devil men raid the neighborhood of so-called Negro women, day and night, to make all desirous of Hell Fire.

This is the way they have planned to beat Allah (God) to the Negroes. What should you do? The answer: Stay away from sweet hearting with devils (the White Race). Surely this is the end of their time, on our planet. Allah said to the devil: "Get out of it despised and driven away. Whoever of them (the Negroes) will follow you, I will certainly fill Hell with you all." (7:18). So, remember, your seeking friendship with this race of devils means seeking a place in their Hell.

The devils swore to them that he was a sincere adviser (7:21). The Holy Qur'an further says: "Surely they took the devils for friends instead of Allah, and they think that they are right guided." (7:30). Not only the Negroes are deceived by this race of Devils, but even many of the Asiatic Muslims do not know that the white race are devils.

Some hate me for teaching this manifest Truth of that race: but, I want my people here (the so-called Negroes) to wake up and escape the fire that Allah has kindled for their enemies (the devils). For, they really are not to blame and only need awakening.

Come to me, my people and I will lead you to your God, and He will set you in Heaven at once!

Hurry and join onto your own kind. Time of This World is At Hand!

OCTOBER 26, 1957 - THE ISLAMIC WORLD

New York Amsterdam News
(Continued from Previous Article)

Since you have been reading in this article, how the devils were made, by being grafted from the Black Nation six thousand years ago; to try them at ruling the original nation of our planet Earth: and that through this grafting, out of that which was originally pure by Nature, it made this grafted race weak physically and wicked mentally.

Some so-called Negroes, who are in love with the devils, do not like to see nor hear them being made manifest. We could lose them without ever missing them; for all who are found believing in and in love with the devils, will be destroyed with the devils.

Now the world must know how to distinguish the real devils from the non-devils; for there are thousands of our people throughout the World who can hardly be distinguished, by color, from the real devil. There are certain climates which seem to change the white race into a "red or brown" color.

And where they mix freely with our own kind, their skin and eyes show a difference in color. Their eyes are brown and grayish blue. By carefully watching their behavior, you can easily distinguish them from our people (dark, brown, yellow or red).

The characteristics of their children are easily distinguished from the original children, regardless to how near in color they may be. The devil children, whenever they are around and among original children, like to show off, and love to make mockery of the original children.

They teach them evil; talk filth; sing filthy songs; filthy dancing and games; and will not leave the original children without starting a fight. Their little mouths, like their parents before them, are filled with cursing and swearing.

No intelligent so-called Negro parent should want their children mixing with white devil children, in school or out. For, they poison your children's minds wherever they are allowed to mix with them. Naturally, they are not like your children. And, their unlikeness attracts your children and yourself.

Remember the Bible's teachings of this race of devils, and especially in II Thessalonians, Chapter (2:3-12) and Revelation (12:9-17, 20:10). The treatment of the so-called Negroes, by the devils, is sufficient proof to the Negroes, that they (the white race) are real devils.

And if this teaching, along with what they are suffering from their beloved devils, does not awaken them to the knowledge of the devils, all I can say for them, then is that they are just lost. They won't be accepted by God nor the righteous Muslims, with even the names of the devils.

Why don't their preachers preach this "vital truth to them," or help me to do so, when the Bible teaches it? Is it a fact that the preachers would rather see their people and themselves suffer at the hands and mouth of this Race, and even go with them to their doom, rather than teach the Truth or help those who are teaching it?

The foolish call the Truth, that I am teaching from the Mouth of God, "Hatred." To tell the Truth cannot be classified as "Hatred" only by those who dislike the Truth.

It is a manifest truth, that white Americans and Europeans hate the so-called Negroes and the whole of black people, the world over; even to the black religious teachers (prophets of the black nation).

RUN DOWN

Let us take a look at the run down on the characteristics of the devils from the Holy Qur'an: "He is in human form (not a spirit) (3:174; 522; 8:48)." "As a leader in unbelief (22:3, 26)." "Standing for wicked opponents (23:97)." "Evil doers are forces of the devils (17:64)." "he (devil) is referred to as Foreign Tribes (38:37)." "As a serpent (37:65)." "he is referred to as, being created from fire (7:12)." "See you from where you can't see them (7:27)." "Has no authority over the righteous (15:42)." "Has no authority, except over those who befriend him (16:99-100)."

"He is one who loves to snoop on the Black Man, to steal a hearing (15:16-18)." "Misleads Adam (2:36; 7:20)." "Leads man to evil (2:36a; 36:62)." "He suggests evil practices (4:119–120)." "Changes the natural religion of man (4:119)." "Gives false promises only to deceive you (14:22)." "Disowns the responsibility for having misled you (14:22; 59:16)." "Sharing in wealth and children (17:64)." "Threatens to mislead the whole of humanity (17:62)."

"Descends upon the sinful (26:221-223)." "The great opposer of Divine Prophets (22:52-53)." "Causing mischief against the righteous (41:36)." "Makes evil deeds look attractive (6:43; 16:63; 27:24; 29:38; 27:4; 35:6–8)." "Struggle of the devils shall fail (4:76)."

You will find all of the above said, to be characteristics of the white race, and you who follow them. But, the black man is not a real devil, only can be a follower of the real devil.

NOVEMBER 2, 1957 - THE ISLAMIC WORLD

New York Amsterdam News

"He, Allah, is One. Allah is He upon whom all depend. He begets not, nor is he begotten, and none is like Him." Holy Qur'an 112: 1-4)

A Muslim is one who believes in ONE God. It is forbidden of Allah (God) for us to believe or serve anyone, other than Himself, as a God. He warns us not to set up an equal with Him: as He was One in the beginning, from whom everything had its beginning: and will be the ONE God from whom everything will end. He is self-independent, having no need of anyone's help, but on the other hand, upon HIM we all depend.

It is the very height of ignorance for us to choose a God or attempt to make something as an equal to Him. For the past 6,000 years, foolish people all over the earth, have been, and are still at it, trying to make an equal to Allah (God).

He has no beginning nor is there any end of Him. How, "Oh, foolish Man," can you make an equal for such ONE? How foolish we make ourselves, serving and worshiping Gods, other than the ONE God, Allah.

The foolish become rich, highly educated in their way and not in the way of Allah (God): and then making and worshiping Gods of their own, the work of their own hands. Then comes the end of them, as it is of today.

ONE GOD

It is the fundamental principle of the religion of Islam to believe in Allah, the ONE GOD. According to the belief, the teaching and preaching of the Prophets of Allah (God) is of One God.

Noah, Abraham, Moses and Jesus – all believed in ONE

GOD (ALLAH). The Christians claim a belief in the above-said Prophets. Then, how do they make Jesus the equal of Allah (God)? The Bible says: "And God spoke all of these words saying, "I am the Lord Thy God. Thou shalt have no other Gods before me.

"Thou shalt not make unto Thee any graven image, or any likeness of anything that is in the Heavens above, or that is in the Earth beneath or that is in the water under the Earth; Thou shalt not bow down Thyself to them, nor serve them, for I the Lord Thy God am a jealous God. "

GOD'S RIVALS

Both Jews and Christians are guilty of setting up rivals to Allah (God). Adam and Eve accepted the guidance of the Serpent, other than Allah (Genesis 3:6). They made and took a golden calf for their God and bowed down to it (Exodus 32:4). This was the work of their own hand to guide them and fight their wars.

The Christians have made imaginary pictures and statues of wood, silver and gold: calling them pictures and statues of God. They bow down to Jesus, His mother and disciples, as though they can see and hear them.

They (the Christians) claim sonship to Allah (God); and take the son to be the equal of the Father; - though they say that, "They killed the Son." Today, they take the weapons of war for their Gods and put their trust in the work of their own hands.

WHY NOT OBEY

Muhammad (May the Peace and Blessings of Allah be upon Him), took hold of the best, the belief in One God (Allah), and was successful. Fourteen hundred years after him, we are successful that is, we who will not set up another God with Allah. The fools who refuse to believe in Allah alone, as the One God, if asked: - "Who made the Heavens and Earth?" They most surely would say God, and would not say: "God the Son, and the Holy Ghost." Then why don't they serve and obey Allah (God)?

It is a perfect insult to Allah (God), who made the Heavens and Earth, and makes the Earth to produce everything for our services, and even the Sun, Moon and Stars – which serve our needs – for us to bow down and worship anything other than Allah as a God. THE GREAT MAHDI, Allah in person, who is in our midst today, will put a stop once and forever, to the serving and worshipping of other Gods besides Himself.

DEVIL'S WAY

It is the Devil's way of bringing the people (the So-Called Negroes) of Allah (God) in opposition to Him, by teaching the people to believe and do just the thing that God forbids. Muhammad (May the Peace and Blessings of Allah be upon Him) did not try making a likeness of God nor have his followers do so.

He and his followers obey and do the law of Allah (the One God), while the Jews and the Christians preach it and do otherwise. We are now being brought face to face with Allah (God), for a showdown between Him and that which we have served as God beside Him.

The Lost and Found members of the Asiatic Nation are especially warned in the 112th Chapter of the Holy Qur'an, against the worship of any other God than Allah. For it is Allah in person, who has found them among the worshippers of Gods other than Allah.

Hurry and lose no time. Join onto your own kind at once.

NOVEMBER 9, 1957 - THE ISLAMIC WORLD

New York Amsterdam News

Why not Islam for all mankind? The answer is simple. All mankind cannot believe and obey the Teachings of Islam. All mankind cannot be members of the Righteous. Islam is righteousness, and he who would believe in it and do the Will of Allah (God) must be, by nature, one born of Allah (God).

The only people born of Allah (God) are the black nation, of whom the so-called American Negroes are descendants, therefore, Islam is offered to them. The white race by nature can't be righteous. Islam was taught to them from Moses to Muhammad, but they were never able to live the life of a believer (Muslim), and can't do it today.

This fact, the so-called American Negroes must learn about the white race: - that they are not of the righteous, unless they could be reborn (grafted back into the black man).

Without this truth, you will forever be deceived by them. This truth will stop the so-called Negroes from begging and looking up to the white race for justice, while they don't do justice by each other.

The poor blind, deaf, and dumb so-called Negroes work hard and live in hope that someday the white race will treat them right: but this will never come to pass – only against the will of that people.

UNITY IS KEY

Certainly, they can do it against their will, but how long will insincere love and justice last? I repeat: "If the so-called American Negroes would try living in unity, have love for self and their own kind (Black man), they would be in Heaven overnight." They work hard to prove to their enemy that they are true and have love for him. This the enemy knows and has known. They (so-called Negroes) never show such sincere love, nor seek it among their own kind where it would be found.

His religion, Islam, will change his mind to thinking right and it is a great job to try and change the so-called Negroes from the ways of their slave masters. It takes much suffering, but it can be done. The white man's religion (Christianity) can't unite us. Instead, it separates us and that is what it was intended to do; divide the people.

KNOW SELF

Know thyself and be yourself: Islam makes a true brother to a brother. The white race, having the knowledge of the black man, took advantage of it: while the black man who was ignorant of the nature of the white race, fell a victim to them.

Now, since you are learning yourself and others, there will certainly come a change in you. Set your face upright to a religion in the right state (Islam). The religion of Islam makes one think in terms of self and one's own kind. This kind of thinking produces an industrious people, self-independent. Christianity does just the opposite. It makes the so-called Negroes lazy, careless, and dependent.

END TO DEPENDENCE

Think over such slavery teaching as this: "a rich man can't see the Hereafter," while Allah (God) is offering the righteous Heaven (riches) while they live. I must continue to warn you, that you can't depend on the white race to care for you forever. There is an end to your dependence on them, so why not start in time seeking something for self?

This is the fall and end of the white race as a dominant power on the earth. Know this, the so-called American Negroes (Tribe of Shabazz): that the loss of Asia to the white race means the end of their luxury, the fall of their riches. It must come to pass, believe it or not. As it is written "Blessed is he who understands."

Hold Unity meetings among yourselves to better your understanding of each other. Whatever your profession or trade, do something for self and your kind; and choose one Religion, Islam. It will secure for you Allah's (God's) favor and protection, and universal brotherhood. The Nation of Islam will be the winner.

ONE MEAL DAILY

Stop looking for anything after Earth: Heaven or Hell. These are conditions of Life. Remember, death settles all. Stop eating yourself to death by eating three and four meals a day. Eat one meal a day and eat the best foods.

By eating right, you enjoy the best of health. Stay away from the hog meat. Don't eat stale meats; chicken or fish. Get fresh meat.

Don't eat field peas, brown or black-eyed peas, nor lima beans. Do not eat collard greens, cabbage sprouts or cornbread. Eat whole wheat bread, all good fruits, plenty of fresh fish, pure butter (if not overweight) and pure cheese. Drink milk and cook your food well done.

Hurry and join onto your own kind.

NOVEMBER 16, 1957 - THE ISLAMIC WORLD

New York Amsterdam News

Let the Scholars of Religions ponder and examine the Sacred pages of their Scriptures, brought by the Prophets of Old, and set aside your prejudices.

Islam is an Arabic word which literally means, "Submission." As the Holy Quran says: "Yea, whoever submits himself entirely to Allah and he is the doer of good to others, he has his reward from his Lord; and there is no fear for him nor shall he grieve." (2:112)

If this is Islam, surely it is the true religion of Allah (God) and His prophets. Entire submission to our Allah (God) is the only way that we could ever hope to obtain His favor. If the other religious believers do not believe in Islam, then we recognize them as nonbelievers in the Divine Supreme Being.

Allah (God) is self-independent, having no need of anything. Can we say the same of ourselves? Since we are not self-independent, then we must be dependent upon Him. Then let us submit to Him, entirely, for help. Nowhere on the Planet Earth does a people need the help of the Divine Supreme Being more than we darker people of America.

Not that we are in great need of food, clothing or money; but protection against a people who will not give us equal justice under their own law.

GODS DIDN'T EXIST

Without Divine help of Allah, we are at the mercy of our enemies. Now that Divine help has come to us, if we only would submit to Him. We submitted to what our enemies taught us, without results, for the Gods that they taught us to serve did not exist.

Jesus, being dead and buried as other Prophets, cannot help us against these enemies of ours, who still hold us in subjection to them. Let us submit to Allah, "There is no fear nor grief."

Fear is the only thing that is preventing us (the so-called Negroes) from being an independent people. Ask yourself this question: "Why do I not have some part of this beautiful Earth that I can call my own as other races and people?" A great number (seventeen million of us in America with two million Indians) not to think of our people living under almost the same condition as we (without equal justice) in the West Indian Islands. Submit to Allah, you and I, for freedom, justice and equality.

No civilized people want the so-called Negroes of America, as a member of their society, in the condition that they are in. Only Allah (God) wants you and me. There is so much work to be done to qualify us (the so-called Negroes). No one, other than Allah and myself, wants the Job but you don't want us, your True Friends.

Islam comes after everything fails. Its significance is the making of peace. The Muslim's greeting to each other is, "Peace." What better religion could we desire after being divided, and made enemies to each other? Don't tell us that you have "Unity and Peace" in the white race's religion called Christianity. The white race does not like Islam, because they can't live the life of freedom, justice, and equality – not even among each other.

NOT INVENTED

Many of you sing that old song, "Give Me That Old Time Religion" – Islam is that "Old Time Religion." It is as old as God Himself; and God is the author of Islam. Islam was not invented as in the case of Christianity and other religions. Islam came with Allah (God) and the universe. In the Holy Qur'an it says: "This day I have perfected for you, your religion and completed my favor on you: and have chosen for you, Islam as a religion."

(5:3)

Here, Islam claims to be a perfect religion; and its author, the perfect one (God). What can be imperfect about Islam when it means, "Entire submission to the will of God?" What can be wrong or imperfect about this religion Islam, which was the religion of Noah, Abraham, Moses, Jesus and all the prophets of God: to Muhammad the last of the prophets?

Islam proves that its author is God, inasmuch that Allah (God) is on the side of every true Muslim.

This is easy to see today. Every one of you, who are accepting Islam in America, can bear me witness that: For the first time in your life, you feel the power and help of Almighty Allah (God) on your side.

LIFE CHANGED

Your whole life becomes a change; one for the better. Your fear is removed; your grief is gone; your desire to continue to do evil things is leaving you for good. Love for your brother (your people) for the first time is now becoming a reality. It is the aim of Allah (God), in giving to you and I, Islam, to unite us and remove fear, sorrow, and sickness; and bring us into that heavenly life, peace of mind, and contentment.

Do you mean to say that you don't need such religion? Or, do you say that the white race's made Christianity is giving you peace and contentment – whose world recognized Father is the Pope of Rome? Not Jesus, nor Allah (God) are the Fathers of the Christian religion, as practiced by the white race, and those who believe in it.

Islam is universally recognized as being the true religion of the Divine Supreme Being. The proof that it is the true religion of God, and that it will get power and friendship for you, with Allah (God) and the righteous – why is the Federal Government and its thousands of agents doing everything in their power, except outright shooting you, to keep you from believing in Allah and his true religion, Islam? They are trying and tricking you in many ways; under the false disguise as now being a friend of yours and wanting to forget the past. But your agreement with them will not stand when you see the showdown.

NATURAL RELIGION

Islam is the natural religion of the black nation. The nature in which they are made; and we are called to return to Islam in these words from the Holy Qur'an: "Set your face upright for religion in the right state. The nature made by Allah in which He has made men: There is no altering of Allah's creation: That is the right religion, but most people do not know." (30:30)

The Devils know the true religion of Allah and have always known it. But, they will not teach it, because it is against their nature to believe and teach the true religion of God, which would upset his chances of ruling the people under falsehood.

Why not Islam? The religion of Islam and its aim will be continued for some time in this article. Hurry and join onto your own kind. The time of this World is at hand.

NOVEMBER 30, 1957 - THE ISLAMIC WORLD

New York Amsterdam News

The Hereafter means after the destruction of the present world, or its power and authority to rule. The Bible and Holy Qur'an Sharrieff are filled with teachings and prophesies on the Hereafter, of which I will leave to you to read for proof.

This subject would not be necessary if it were not for that "Man of Sin" being permitted to rule. Since he (The Devil) was given authority to rule us for six thousand years, the word "hereafter" is used, meaning: - After the "Man of Sin," because his (The Devils') time was limited to a certain time, six thousand years. Some say, after the Judgement when the man of sin and his people have been judged and the death sentence executed.

May I say here, that: This present world was sentenced to death when the "Man of Sin" was made, and all who follow him. The Holy Qur'an says: "Whoever of Them will follow you, I will certainly fill Hell with you all." (7:18)

The Bible says: "These both were cast alive into a lake of fire." (Revelation 19:20) The "Man of Sin," and his people, deceived the righteous by making them believe that he (Devil) was also one of the Righteous. They claim that all are from one Father (the same God), while that is not true. (The God Righteousness is not the God of Evil.)

We all look forward to seeing the hereafter and living under a ruler of justice and a Government of Righteousness, after the destruction of the unrighteousness. The "Man of Sin" (the devils) are now worried, disgusted, and dissatisfied with their own Rule and Rulers, and wish for a change to a better World: but they desire to be the Rulers in the better World.

The hereafter, some believe, is after the great war of Armageddon, or holy war, which is a religious war between the two great religions of the earth and their believers, namely:

Islam and Christianity. Of course, Buddhism will also be involved.

ISLAM TYPICAL

In the hereafter, the righteous will make an unlimited progress. Peace, joy, and happiness will have no end. War will be forgotten: disagreement will have no place in the hereafter. The present Brotherhood of Islam is typical of the life in the hereafter.

The only difference will be that the Brotherhood in the hereafter will enjoy the spirit of gladness and happiness, forever, in the presence of Allah. The people (the Muslims) will make such a change that the people will think that they have a new earth. It will be the Heaven of the righteous.

NO SICKNESS

No sickness, hospitals, insane asylums, gambling, cursing, and swearing will ever be seen nor heard in that life. Decay, fear, grief, and sorrow will stop on this side as proof. Every one of the so-called Negroes, who accept the religion of Islam, and follow what Allah has revealed to me, will begin enjoying the above life, NOW!

I have never felt like this before. Islam is Heaven for you and me. They (Muslims) can see their God in Truth. The righteous Muslims will meet and embrace you in peace (As-Salaam-Alaikum).

The life in the hereafter is an image of the spiritual state of this life. Just think how good you feel when in the divine spirit for a while. You are so happy that you do not feel even the pain of sickness, trouble, or sorrow. That is the way you will always feel, in the hereafter.

No eyes have seen, nor ears have heard what Allah has in store for those Muslims who see the hereafter. There are so many beautiful teachings on this subject in the Holy Qur'an, that one could write books on it.

NOW IS TIME

We, the so-called Negroes who accept Allah and Islam, will reap that glorious joy and happiness. You will be clothed in silk, interwoven with gold; and you will eat the best of food. Whatever you desire. Now is the time when you can enter that life, for your God is here in person to bring it to pass. You will never be that which you cannot be anymore. Just believe in Him.

You have been deceived by the Archdeceiver (the Devil) in regard to the hereafter. You are made to believe that the hereafter is a life of spirits (spooks) somewhere in the sky, while the hereafter is only here on the Earth. And, we will not become spirit beings. The life in the hereafter is only a continuation of our present life. You will be flesh and blood.

There will be no spooks coming up out of graves to meet God. That is not true. The physically dead person will not be in the hereafter. That is slavery belief, taught by the slave masters, to keep you blind, deaf, and dumb so that they can rule you.

They make you believe in a Heaven after death. The slave master knows that death settles it all, and that you will not return to tell him whether he lied or told the truth. Read the Scriptures carefully on the life in the hereafter.

Try to understand it, and you will find that it actually does not mean what you have been made to believe. No one is going to leave this Planet to live on another. One could not even if one wanted to and tried. You cannot reach the moon and live on it: so be satisfied and believe in Allah. Live where you are – on your "Good Earth" – but be the righteous.

I must quote these beautiful verses here, from the Holy Qur'an. It says: "O Soul that is at rest, return to your Lord, well pleased with Him, well pleasing. So, enter among my Servants and enter into my Paradise." (89:27-30).

Hurry and lose not time in joining onto your own kind. The time of this world is at hand.

DECEMBER 7, 1957 - THE ISLAMIC WORLD

New York Amsterdam News

The great mistake so-called Negroes make is: believing that the God who is their Father is the same God and Father of the White Race. **NOT SO:** Neither Jesus, nor Moses before Jesus accepted the Caucasian Race as being the people of the Divine Supreme Being.

You are hard-hearted and in great love with your open enemies. You despise Almighty Allah (God) for not loving them as you; and refuse to accept His only True Religion (Islam) just because you have learned that God will not accept any devil (white) races in His Kingdom.

Therefore, you stay out of the Holy Nation of Islam, thinking that you are on the side of power (the white race) and that Allah and His people (the Muslims) are weak. But, you shall soon know who is the weaker in power.

Know that whatever is in the Heavens and earth is Allah's and Allah gives power to whom He pleases, as Jesus said (John 8:42) "If the God of the white race is the same God of the black nation, you would love each other." You sincerely love the white race because you are made blind, deaf, and dumb by them. Therefore, your love of them is due to your blindness and your inability to see them as the real devils.

UNABLE TO SEE

Being unable to see and distinguish the truth from falsehood you are deaf to the truth; and dumb to the speaking of the truth. As a result, the devils are making merchandise out of you. The white race (the devils), as I have shown you so many times in this article, were created an enemy to all black mankind: not a friend of the God of righteousness. They are great deceivers, murderers, robbers, and filthy tempters of the black nation.

Could their evil God be your Father? Could Adam and Eve be the black man's parents when it was the black people who chased them out of Paradise? Could Adam be our father when we have no birth record, but Adam has. He was born six thousand years ago. Would you accept Adam as your father whom God rejected and sent out into the worst part of our Planet (Europe and America) to live their 6,000 years?

Never say anymore that Adam is your father. You have no part whatsoever in the white race. Do not hope to take part with them, that is, if you know what is good for you.

DEVILS

Read and study the above Chapter of St. John 8:42-44, you who are Christian believers in the Bible and Jesus, as you say. If you understand it right, you will agree with me that the whole Caucasian Race is a race of devils. They were proven to be devils in the garden of Paradise and condemned four thousand years later by Jesus. Likewise, they are condemned today as the same, by the **GREAT MAHDI MUHAMMAD**, as being nothing but devils in the plainest language that even a fool can understand.

The so-called American Negroes have been deceived and blinded by their unlikeness; soft, smooth buttered words; eye winking; back patting; false show of friendship, and hand shaking. Such acts mentioned above, with the exception of handshaking by men, is a disgrace to any decent, intelligent person. **KNOW THE TRUTH and** be **FREE** of such disgrace to you.

Write and join onto your own kind. The time of this World is at hand.

DECEMBER 14, 1957 - THE ISLAMIC WORLD

The Destruction of Integration
New York Amsterdam News
(Continued from Previous Article)

Allah has revealed the Truth. He is not going to beg you or me to accept it. He is Self-Independent. The Christian Church begs the people to join the church. There is quite a difference between the two people, Black and White, and their religions (Islam and Christianity). In this column I have told and am still trying to tell my people the Truth. Nothing Else! I am willing to pay with my life if found lying: for I give to you that which has been revealed to me from the Author of Truth, Allah, the Lord of you and me. If you believe, it will be good for you; disbelieve and try opposing it, and you will suffer shame and disgrace.

Not one so-called American Negro should want to integrate with his slave master's children; for a day is near that you will wish that the distance between you and them was as the East is from the West. I have taught and do continue to teach you, just who you are and who the white race is. Almighty God Allah has given to me a clear knowledge of the beginning and end of this devil race.

Why do you want a proud devil, when God most surely will destroy them? Why do you want to sit or stand near them? Why do you want your little children going in the same schools tougher, as long as your children can be taught the same textbook by a teacher of his Nation?

AGAINST NATURE

As free slaves, you should not accept anything but being separated from white people, who have and still treat you worse than a dog. Do you want to be like them? Just why do you want the devils for your husbands and wives? Integrating will produce more spotted children. It is against Nature.

Look at the black mother nursing a little half-white baby from her dark breast, and a white mother nursing a little black baby from her white breast. Does it look natural to you or does it look odd? Not by any means does it look natural. Even the very nature of the two mothers makes them feel that they are out of their places with their own kind.

As I was driving on the streets the other day, I saw a black girl sitting in the front seat of a car near the driver who was white. When the two saw me looking at them, both looked guilty. Both knew that they were out of their own places and nature made them bear witness in their looks that they were wrong.

DESTROYED SLAVES

The white race has already destroyed its black slaves. They have more colors than all the people of the earth combined: yet you are not ashamed of this disgraceful, illegitimate practice in your families by the children of your slave masters. If God had wanted black and white to be mixed, He would not have made them two distinct people. God forbid!

Do you want such people to be your own? If they will do such among themselves, what will they do to you, and especially your girls and women. What do you think is happening with your daughter or your wife, who is out there sweet hearting with the devils day and night and never says or makes a cry that she was attacked by one of these inhuman beasts?

I appeal to you my brothers and sisters of the Black Nation: let us unite in the name of Allah (God) and put a stop to this destruction of our nation through our women, for God forbids your integration with them. There will never be any good coming out of it. Seek unity among your own first.

AS IT'S WRITTEN

As it is written, "You are the best of the Nations, raised up for the benefit of men, you enjoin what is right, and forbid the wrong and believe in Allah: and if the followers of the book (The Christians: the book, "The Bible") had believed, it would have been better for them, they shall by no means harm you but with a slight evil; and if they fight with you they shall turn their backs to you, then shall they not be helped; they have become deserving of wrath from Allah, and humiliation is made to cleave to them; this is because they disbelieved in the communications of Allah, and slew the prophets unjustly." (Holy Qur'an 3:109, 111.)

The White Christian Race is referred to here as being deserving of the wrath of God; for they killed the prophets of God, opposed them and their Messages of Allah, as they are doing to me today with you as their helpers.

The Bible also charges this race of devils with killing God's Prophets, "O Jerusalem, Jerusalem, thou that killest the prophets and stonest them which are sent unto thee." (Matthew 23:27)

Will you make love with a people who do not love Allah (God) and kills God's prophets and persecutes you and me if we ask or seek Justice for ourselves and our Nation? Will you aid them against your own black brother!

Write and join onto your own kind. The time of this World is at hand.

DECEMBER 21, 1957 - THE ISLAMIC WORLD

New York Amsterdam News

While teaching and representing a religion to you called "Islam." The most important thing to do is to answer the questions: "What is Islam? Who is the Author? Who are its Prophets and people? Such questions could be answered in a few words and one can make books out of the answers.

Briefly, "Islam" means entire submission to the will of Allah (God). It is moreover, a significant name. Its primary significance is the making of peace and the idea of "peace" is the dominant idea in Islam.

The Author of Islam is Allah (God). We just cannot imagine God being the Author of any other religion but one of peace. Since peace is the very nature of Allah (God), and peace He seeks for His people, and peace is the nature of the righteous, most surely Islam is the religion of peace.

It is the religion offered to the people to bring about a peace of mind and contentment after destroyers of peace with falsehoods have been destroyed. The entire creation of Allah (God) is of peace, not including the devils who are not the creation of Allah (God) but a race created by an enemy (Yakub) of Allah.

Yakub rebelled against Allah and the righteous people and was cast out of the homes of the righteous into the worst part of our planet to live their way of life until the fixed day of their doom.

PROPHETS LISTED

These enemies of Allah (God) are known at the present time as the white race or European race, who are the sole responsible people for misleading nine-tenths of the total population of the black nation.

The prophets of Islam include: Noah, Abraham, Moses, Jesus, Job, David, Solomon and Jonah. The people of Islam are the Black People, and their members are made up of the Brown, Yellow and Red people called races. The book of Islam is the Holy Qur'an Sharrieff, and the scriptures that were brought by the above-mentioned prophets were of Islam.

The Bible does not mention Islam by name as the religion of the Prophets; nor does it give us the name of any of the Divine Prophets' religions. By not teaching the reader the name of the former Prophets' religions yet giving the name Christianity to what Jesus taught, it leaves the reader to seek the name of the religion of the former Prophets from Adam to Muhammad.

The followers or believers of Islam are over one-half billion people. Even among the infidels you will find many to confess to Islam, although by nature they are against Islam. If I teach or preach a religion claiming its origin is from Allah (God), I must prove it: and if you oppose it with another religion which you claim God to be its Author, then you must prove your claim.

A religion whose origin or roots cannot be found in the Universal order of God cannot be said to be the religion of God. The first prophet of God and His Scripture must be that of the true religion of God.

FIVE PRINCIPLES

Islam has five fundamental principles of belief. The most essential of them all is "The belief in ONE GOD." This was the belief (Oneness of God) and preaching of the prophets of God from Noah to Muhammad (the last). As I said: "if your religion's roots are not found in the universal order of things it is not from Allah (God).

I will prove in this column, from time to time, that Islam has its roots in [DM1]the Universal order (God's Creation) of things. I also will prove that Islam is mathematics and that mathematics is Islam: and will defy my opposer, Rev. George C. Violenes, to prove that the religion (as we know it today) called Christianity to be the religion of God and His prophets: Noah, Abraham, Lot, Moses, David and Jesus.

CHRIST NO CHRISTIAN

I am at a loss to know just why the Rev. Violenes in his first two columns is reading to us the history of Abraham as recorded by the Bible writers. There is nothing in the way of defense for Christianity, for Abraham was not a Christian. He was a Muslim prophet, and according to history, I can prove it. And, will prove that Jesus was not a Christian nor the founder of the so-called Christian Religion.

In his second article, he mentioned the history of Moses and Muhammad. He referred to me as calling the Caucasian Race (the white race) Devils: and hints that the treatment which the Jews received under Pharaoh was far worse than that received by our fathers and their children under the Caucasians of America.

He even said that: "Moses' mission was basically the foundation of Christianity and Islam." Moses was a prophet of Islam. But, where is any base in Moses' mission for so-called Christianity? Rev. Violenes, I eagerly await you to prove my preaching of being other than the Truth.

Write and Join onto your own kind. The time of this world is at hand.

DECEMBER 28, 1957 - THE ISLAMIC WORLD

New York Amsterdam News

"Say: O People of the Book, come to an equitable word between us and you, that we shall serve none but Allah and that we shall not associate aught with Him, and that some of us shall not take others for lords besides Allah. But if they turn away, then say: Bear witness, we are Muslims. O People of the Book, why do you dispute about Abraham, when the Torah and the Gospel were not revealed till after him? Do you not understand?" Holy Qur'an (3:64-65)

The Jews and Christians both take Abraham be the father of their religion or faith while Abraham was before both Moses and Jesus. Moses brought the Torah, Jesus brought the (Injil) Gospel, Abraham was an Arab Muslim and not a Jew nor a Christian. Says the Holy Qur'an: "Abraham was not a Jew nor a Christian, but he was an upright man, a Muslim, and he was not one of the polytheists." (Chapter 3:66).

A Muslim is an upright person, a believer in ONE GOD (not three). The Jews and the Christians both agree that Abraham was a believer in one God. The Christians cannot take Abraham as a father of their faith because the Christian's faith or religion is a belief in three Gods: Father, Son and Holy Ghost. This kind of belief is called Polytheism, and this the true name for all Christians.

Abraham submitted to Allah (God) to serve and obey Him. The Jews nor the Christians never have submitted entirely to Allah (God) nor Moses and Jesus to do righteousness. Do you say they have when the Jews and the Christians are charged with killing the Prophets of God?

It is a manifest proof that the Prophets' religion was Islam (submission to the will of Allah (God)). Surely the Jews and the Christians would not have killed the Prophets if the Prophets were of their own religions: (Judaism and Christianity).

Abraham is mentioned throughout the Holy Qur'an as being a Muslim.

FEARED BY WHITES

Of all the religions of the world, Islam is hated and feared most by the white man and especially for the so-called Negroes. "And when his Lord tried Abraham with certain words, he fulfilled them. He said: Surely I will make you a leader of men." (Holy Qur'an 2:124)

Abraham submitted to the Will of Allah and became the recipient of we the lost-found members of our nation. "And We said unto Abram, know of a surety that thy seed shall be a stranger in a land that I not theirs and shall serve them; and afflict them for 400 years."

The seed of Abraham has been much of a controversy but we do know today who the seed of Abraham is. No people fit the description better than the American so-called Negroes. They have been here in the midst of strangers (white race) for around four hundred years in a land that is not theirs. They now are a Nation of little over seventeen million.

And, out of the forty-eight states of America, they do not own one state, and never have demanded one. Of all the races and Nations of earth, the so-called Negroes are the most satisfied with nothing but a job. Their many leaders never sought a country for their enslaved brothers or demanded to be returned to their native land and people.

PREPARING PLACE

Allah is now preparing a place for them. "And who has a better religion than he who submits himself entirely to Allah? And is a doer of good and follows the faith of Abraham, the upright one, and Allah took Abraham as a friend." (Holy Qur'an 4:125). And in another place: "And who forsake the religion of

Abraham but he who makes himself a fool. When his Lord said to him, submit, he said I submit myself to the Lord of the Worlds." (Chapter 2: 131, 132)

And the same did Abraham enjoin on his sons, "O my sons, surely Allah has chosen for you this faith (Islam) therefore die not unless you are Muslims." (Same Chapter, Verse 132)

"O followers of the book (Bible) why do you confound the truth with falsehood and hide the truth while you know?" (Holy Qur'an 3:70). The Jews and the Christians are most certainly guilty of the above charge of hiding the truth even though they know it. Nothing but the devil will do such a thing.

Hurry and join onto your own kind The Time of this World is at Hand.

JANUARY 4, 1958 – THE ISLAMIC WORLD

New York Amsterdam News

I first get the impression that my opponent, Rev. Violenes, wanted to defend the religion called Christianity. But, according to his articles for the past three weeks, he seems to be trying to defend the White Race (which is natural for Black Preachers) from being called by their own name (Devils); which they (the White Race) do not try to defend.

I want the Rev. Violenes to tell us just who are the made devils if the white race is not the devils? Where did the white race come from? Who is the father?

If the Rev. Violenes agrees with me on the Revelation of Allah that the white race were the cave people of Europe 4,000 years ago, where were they before that? What caused them to be in such condition (the caves)?

Rev. Violenes further says in the same article that I said: "The so-called Negroes have suffered under this white man's Christianity and are lynched, their churches and homes burned." Does the Reverend mean to say that it is not true? The suffering that these devils have put upon my people have no parallel in history. John Hawkins, the first slave trader was a Christian.

The Bible and Holy Qur'an mention Pharaoh as killing the babies of their slaves and adding to their labor in the time of Moses, and denying them the freedom to pray and worship their own God (Jehovah). This added burden to the slave seems to have taken place just prior to and after the birth of Moses, but no lynching and drunkenness.

Moses was born two thousand years after the creation of the devils (the white race) and two thousand years before Jesus. Moses lifted the white race out of the caves of Europe. This is mentioned in the Bible (John 3:14).

FROM GOD

Rev. Violenes admits at the end of this same article, that Muhammad taught his people to abandon their polytheistic tribal and religious customs and to believe in the One True God. Rev. Violenes has been representing the Prophets of Allah and Islam from the start of his writing: Abraham, Moses, Jesus, and Muhammad (May the peace and blessings of Allah be upon them). He has as yet to tell us with proof, who is the founder of Christianity, (the belief in three Gods).

In his article of December 21, 1957, the Rev. Violenes seems to be running out of material to defend Christianity, and focused his attack on me and my so-called limited education and knowledge.

My answer to that can be read in both the Bible and Holy Qur'an: Mine is from God and yours is from the devils, just as Abraham and the Prophets after him (Muhammad the last) had no education. Yet, after 1,376 years, one-fifth of the population of the Earth are their followers. Muhammad was not born in an ox stall, nor did the angels make any mistake of saying "Peace and Good Will to mankind," before they had gotten rid of the peace breakers; nor was there any announcing of putting up the sword before it had conquered the enemy.

Read your Bible and the Holy Qur'an. They will teach you and me what type of man God will choose to deliver His last message. His choice certainly did not fall on the proud Christian preachers. If my education was from the devils, I would love them and preach against Allah and His Religion and make mockery of His Prophets as you and they are doing. And, accuse God of adultery by getting a son by Mary and bowing down worshipping images of wood, stone and various metals of her and her son throughout the Western World.

SALVATION

Islam is the salvation of the black Man! Rev. Violenes says Christianity is not only the hope of the Negroes, but of the World. Let him prove it! The so-called Negro who accepts Islam does not have to go to Court and fight the teachers and the Muslims to get them to recognize him as brother.

He is received as one of the family. He walks and talks with the King and they both pray together under the same roof. Rev. Violenes is in great love with our enemies (the white race) and fears our enemies more than he fears God. Reverend, you cannot hope to Baptize me in the name of the prophet sent to the Jews. I am baptized in the One (Allah) Who sent Moses and Jesus, and I need no water baptism; I take that every morning in my bath tub.

I was born baptized in the "Spirit of Allah." I need no rebirth. I also was born a Muslim by nature and not self-styled. The only ones who will have to be reborn to see the Hereafter, is you White People, whom you are trying to defend as being members of the righteous. Their flesh and blood cannot see the Hereafter and this they will agree with me.

I will never pray to Jesus who was sent to the Jews 2,000 years ago and who is dead and cannot hear a prayer. The poor so-called Negroes are made to believe such lies from the cradle without any proof: That a God is somewhere in space listening or watching for them.

And, that Jesus of 2,000 years ago is sitting at His right hand waiting until the Judgment to return with his wounded body by the Roman officers to show that he is the same Jesus. This is the worst lie ever told. Where is that heaven they are in? Point it out to us! Prove that Jesus is still alive! Your Bible is a fixed book by the enemies (Devils).

I understand it, but from what you have and still are saying shows that you really do not understand it. I wish the Amsterdam Newspaper would put someone in your place who knows the science of the Bible and the White Mans' Religion called Christianity and the Religion of God and His Prophets; and not a man who just likes to read to us the Bible without knowledge of what he is reading.

There is no defense for a false religion in the Book of God and His Prophets. Condemn me with Truth, not mere words of dislike for me and what I am teaching because of your love for our enemies or get your teacher to try doing so.

Hurry and join onto your own kind. The Time of this World is at Hand.

JANUARY 11, 1958 — THE ISLAMIC WORLD

New York Amsterdam News

Reverend Violenes said that "Jesus Christ is the Prince of Peace, and that it was fulfilled nearly two thousand years ago." (Isaiah 9:6). We want him to prove it!

What Jesus Christ is the Prince of Peace? The World history bears me witness that there has been more dissatisfaction, disagreements, revolutions, and wars since the birth and death of Jesus than ever before.

Today, all the civilized nations of Earth are dissatisfied, and have been and are preparing to destroy each other in a final war; which they call Holy War or the Third World War. Since 1914, the Christians started the last two World Wars and are now starting the Third and last World War.

What Jesus Christ is the Prince of Peace? Can we give Jesus credit for something that he did not do? Or, would you like to be called a Preacher of lies?

Isaiah 9:6 nor Galatians 4:4 cannot be referring to the Prophet Jesus two-thousand years ago, for we are witnesses that this world is not enjoying peace. History teaches us that there has not been any peace in the world since the civilization of the white race; and that there will not be any peace until their ruling power has been destroyed.

ONLY PEACE

The only peace that History shows which the Black Nation has enjoyed in the past six-thousand years, was the two-thousand years that the white race was in the hills and cave sides of the present continent called Europe. The past four-thousand years have been written in war and bloodshed.

Jesus came two-thousand years after Moses, and was

killed by the sword. Although, according to the Bible, he did not come to bring peace. (Matthew 10:34). Therefore, the sword was the victor of his time.

I am ashamed for Reverend Violenes, who calls himself a representative of the word of God and does not know the word of God. The sword killed Jesus and his disciples, whom you call the "Prince of Peace." Isaiah 9:6 does not mention Jesus Christ by name. It calls the one who will bring about peace: "The Mighty God, the everlasting Father."

"The Mighty God, the everlasting Father" cannot refer to Jesus, since you say that Jesus was the son of God. The seventh verse of the same chapter says: "Of the increase of his government and peace there shall be no end. Justice from henceforth even forever, the zeal of the Lord of hosts will perform this."

For the past two-thousand years, this prophesied government of peace and justice has not arrived. So, it must be God, himself, whom Isaiah 9:6-7 is referring to, and not a prophet of the past four-thousand years.

DISCOUNTS CALENDAR

Reverend Violenes wants us to use the dates and calendars of the people to determine the age of a religion. Such ignorance! The age and birth of a religion must be determined by the principles of belief, or faith that make that religion. And, by the scriptures or revelation of the prophets.

According to the Holy Qur'an, Muhammad was no the founder of Islam, nor were even the prophets before him the founders. It says: "Surely we have revealed to you as we revealed to Noah and the prophets after him, Abraham, Ishmael, Isaac, Jacob, and the Tribes, Moses and Job, Jonah, Aaron, David, Solomon, Jesus. (Holy Qur'an 4:163).

It further says: "This day I have perfected for you your

religion – and completed my favor on you and chosen for you Islam as a religion." (Holy Qur'an 5:3). Therefore, Muhammad, nor the prophets before him can truthfully be said to have been the founders of Islam.

Hurry and join onto your own kind. The Time of this World is at Hand.

JANUARY 18, 1958 - THE ISLAMIC WORLD

New York Amsterdam News

Reverend Violenes desires to keep the so-called Negroes a slave for their White Masters by reading off the Bible (Poison Book) to them without true interpretation, last week, as in the beginning of his articles; trying to defend the White Race and their slave making religion called Christianity, with the prophets of Islam and their scriptures, who are believers in One God.

Also, last week, he desired that the public believe as he believers. (Perhaps by pointing out to us such Bible scripture as Isaiah 42:8, 44:6). These prophecies refer to the work of the One God among the so-called American Negroes in these last days of this wicked world of the White Race, of which the Prophet Isaiah foresaw.

Let the public read and study the sayings of those scriptures that Reverend Violenes is trying to use as proof for the base of the Christian Religion; a belief in three Gods. He must remember that the former Prophets did not dare to set up equals with Allah, the One God. "I am the Lord; that is My Name and My Glory will I not give to another, neither My praise to graven images." (Isaiah 42:8).

The very first verse of this chapter to the tenth, cannot be referring to Jesus nor any of the Prophets in the past. It is a prophecy of the Last Chosen Messenger of Allah (God) in the last days.

NO SON MENTIONED

No son is mentioned. This is a servant. He is an elect. God is pleased with him and has put His spirit on him (taught him Divine Wisdom). With the Divine Truth received from God, he will bring about the judgment of the Gentiles (disbelievers in Allah).

God shall uphold him (protect him). "His voice is not heard

in the streets, "cannot be referring to Jesus. He preached in the streets, on hillsides, and sea shores. "He shall not cry," Jesus wept. (St. John 7:37, 11:35). "He shall not fail, nor be discouraged, till he has set Judgment in the Earth." Jesus failed to convert the Jews, nor did he set the prisoners free of the powers of darkness of the falsehood of this World of Satan.

PRISONER-CONVERTS

The world of Allah, revealed to me, is now being preached in nearly every prison house in the country. Prisoners are becoming converts to Islam throughout America. Ask the wardens! Islam is turning them to righteousness; making them righteous people for the first time in their lives. The church and her religion, Christianity, cannot stop the people from drinking intoxicating drinks, gambling, dope, tobacco, eating the hog and hatred for each other.

But, Islam is doing it. The whole of the 42nd Chapter of Isaiah refers to God's Servant and His protection for that Servant in the last days. The 19th verse teaches us that the Servant was one from among the blind, deaf and dumb, and he was missioned to open their eyes and ears. Jesus was not blind, deaf and dumb.

Reverend Violenes does not know the 99 attributes of Allah (God). The White Race has kept the so-called Negroes blind, deaf and dumb to the knowledge of Allah, Islam, and its Prophets. Therefore, the name of Allah has never been taught to them. The name "ALLAH" is the 100th attribute. The word "God" is limited. It only means power and force.

CITES BIBLE "ERRORS"
The mention of an angel being the equal of God (Exodus 3:2, 5) is a mistake. The Bible has many errors in it, caused by those who translated it. I do not see how the Reverend Violenes could write such contrary scripture for the base of Christianity. The Qur'an (41:6) declares that: "There is no God but Allah, the first and the last," which is direct teachings of Islam. God has

not and never will accept a people who make His angels His equal.

Reverend Violenes says that: "The work of the father is distinct while the son is vividly seen, and the Holy Spirit is not seen but felt." Then there is no equal. Without the first (Father) there is no second nor third. Therefore, a belief in the father of all is a belief in the other two. But, we cannot make the other two equals with their creator, for the second two creations were dependent on the father. "Allah is One God. He has no equal, and there is none like Him. He has no associate." Is the creature equal to its Creator?

Reverend Violenes, is this Jesus of Matthew 28:19 the same one of Matthew 10:5,6 who sent his disciples only to the lost sheep of the House of Israel and told them not to go to the Gentiles or in any city of Samaritans? If so, what changed his mind towards those forbidden areas?

Hurry and join onto your own kind. The Time of this World is at Hand.

JANUARY 25, 1958 - THE ISLAMIC WORLD

New York Amsterdam News

Of all the Saints' and prophets' deaths, there is more confusion over whether Jesus is dead or living than any man that ever lived on our Planet Earth. Why? I will proceed to show you just why.

The past Jesus' history, of two-thousand years ago, was a sign of something to come. As the Holy Qur'an says: "And we made the son of Mary and his mother a sign." (23:50) Not very long ago, I made it clear in this article to whom the sign referred.

It refers to the Great Mahdi (God in person) and His marvelous work among the lost-found (the so-called Negroes) members of the black nation. Restoring the lost knowledge and uniting the so-called Negroes again on to their own kind (Nation) and country, is like giving life to a physical death.

This Great Mahdi is God in person; and is also, the answer to the prophecy of the coming of Jesus. There is a great difference between the two men and their work. The former Jesus was unable to convert the Jews to whom he was sent. On the other hand, the Mahdi (God in person) will convert the whole of the lost-found so-called Negroes. He will even use His first convert to convert the rest; and through this one, He will open the eyes of the World to that which has been hidden from them. I am His first convert.

There is much to be said here to verify the above, but the wise of you will understand; as I am not writing here a book, but rather an article.

JESUS NOT ALIVE

Jesus of two-thousand years ago cannot be alive in some place. We cannot agree with the Bible nor Holy Qur'an or any other book that says he is yet alive. If we understand what these scriptures actually mean, we cannot disagree with them.

Neither the Holy Qur'an nor the Bible tells us what Jesus and his mother were a sign of. That is done for protection, and to serve as a test between the knowledge of the believers and disbelievers in the last days of this world. There is no record of anyone, regardless of how good or bad they were, coming to life after being dead and buried—before Jesus nor since Jesus.

Just what purpose would Jesus have served two-thousand years ago for God to have allowed him to suffer death and bring him back to life, and then hide him from the Public's eyes until the end of the world? God never speaks nor does a work without a purpose. Again, why should God love Jesus more than any other of His prophets while Jesus was unable to convert the Jews (to whom he was missioned) to Him?

Moses' grave has not been found nor has Moses been seen by the World since his death; nor any of the former prophets. Abraham was one of the beloved prophets, but we have not seen him risen from his death.

May I help you to understand as God has revealed it to me? The resurrection of Jesus, from the dead, is now going on among the so-called Negroes, who are spiritually dead to the Divine knowledge of Self and God. The first Jesus was born among the spiritually dead Jews or to be more correct, among a race whose death was fixed on the day of their creation.

The difference in the two (Negroes' and Jews' death) is: The Jews or white race in general, receives a total death at the end of six-thousand years because of being created wicked, and enemies of God from the beginning. They cannot be reformed into righteous people.

DIVINE FAMILY

The so-called Negroes are members of the Divine family (Nation) of God, whose fall and death came from being deceived by the white race or Adamic People, and who can now, and are being resurrected and restored to their original place among the Righteous (their own Nation) and will live forever.

Hurry and join unto your own kind. The Time of This World Is At Hand.

FEBRUARY 1, 1958 - THE ISLAMIC WORLD

New York Amsterdam News

Neither Jesus nor any former prophet can be questioned after their death. We only can seek our answer from their histories. Chapter 3, Verse 117, of the Holy Qur'an can easily be misunderstood; that is, if we are more inclined to believe that Jesus is still alive. There is a live Jesus today, but not the one of two thousand years ago.

The Holy Qur'an says that Jesus said: "When Thou didst cause me to die." It leaves no doubt in the mind of the reader that Jesus is really dead, and no one can be questioned after their death concerning the things of their life.

The above words could have been said by him while he was living, and a record made of them; but let us remember; Allah will question his last Apostle in the last days (at the Judgment) of just how he delivered His message, and how the people received him.

This last Apostle will be alive when questioned by Allah, and he it is who is the real fulfiller of the former prophets' histories: Abraham, Moses, Jesus and Muhammad. That man, God will raise from the mentally dead so-called Negroes.

CITES VERSES

The 119th and 120th Verses of this Chapter show that the questioning will take place in the Judgment of this world in these words: "This is the day when their truth shall benefit the truthful ones; Allah is well pleased with them and they are well pleased with Allah."

There are many things prophesied of the future under many other names other than the real one. This is done to protect the real one. I could say much on this subject, but you would not believe it although it is the truth, and the days of the manifestation of the truth.

I seek refuge in Allah, the Lord of the Dawn (the Dawn of the Light of Truth) from the evil of these (Yakub's made devils), who have destroyed the peace of the entire Nations of Earth; who invited the whole Civilized World to evil, indecency and bloodshed.

GREAT DECEIVERS

The Great Deceivers—the enemies of Allah and His Prophets, and all Black Nations of Earth—haters and murderers of my people the so-called Negroes; but they would not like that the Negroes hate and murder them.

The White Race teaches the so-called Negroes to love their enemies, which they cannot do themselves, nor even God. But, they really have made the so-called Negroes to love them and hate their own kind. No civilized people of Earth loves their enemies.

The frightened and cowardly so-called Negroes try hiding themselves behind the falsehoods put in the Bible by the slave masters (Luke 6:27-29) and claim it to be Jesus teachings. Could Jesus have prophesied the destruction of the devils, the enemies of God; and then teach us to love the enemies of God and the righteous? It says in John 4:4; "Whosoever therefore will be a friend of the world is the enemy of God."

KNOWS ENEMIES

The Holy Qur'an is also bitterly against having friendship with the enemies of God. Brother Sheikh Daoud Ahmed Faisal knows the enemies of Allah, but from the sympathetic words made in this newspaper for them in the January 19, 1958 issue in regard to their slavery making religion called Christianity, shows Mr. Faisal to be part believer in both Christianity and Islam.

Mr. Faisal charged me with not giving "Justice" to Islam in my defense of Islam and my people, (the American so-called Negroes) against a preacher of the religion (Christianity) that has and is still holding my people in a mentally slavish condition; of whom Allah and myself are trying and will free by laying bare the false teacher and his religion (Christianity).

I desire that Mr. Faisal show one word of fact that I have said that can be proven as an injustice to Islam? My people here in America will have to be taught first, a thorough knowledge of "Self" and their enemies before they can or will accept strict Islam. That knowledge they are receiving from Allah through me whom He missioned. Can a savage first be taught the science of good society before he is taught to wear clothes?

Hurry and join onto your own kind. The time of this world is at hand.

FEBRUARY 8, 1958; — THE ISLAMIC WORLD

New York Amsterdam News

No civilized Nation wants the so-called Negroes, but Allah, our Loving and Most Merciful God, Who came in the person of Master Fard Muhammad in 1930. It was not until 1933 did He begin revealing His true self; I knew Him at first sight in 1931, for I was expecting Him.

The devils knew Him and are in pain because of Him; not to mention the Holy wise Scientists of Islam. They will never acquaint the Negroes with Him, nor will they ever tell you anything of good that is in your favor. If all of their enemy nations were closing in on them, here in Chicago, Illinois, they would not tell you until you saw them.

Mr. Emmanuel Rosenfeld of New York, who fears that my articles in this paper (which teaches my people the truth) will stir up hatred in the hearts of my people towards the White people would like to see my articles discontinued. Let us ask Mr. Rosenfeld, who stirred up hatred of the so-called American Negroes?? The Bible says, "Do unto others as you would like others to do unto you." This mistreatment of our people by the Caucasian Race will be given back to them in full. A token of it is now going on.

I am not the least concerned what the white race believes in as a religion. They are not my people nor are we their people, nor is our God the same. I am never surprised to see or hear of evils committed by white people. The only time that they would surprise me is on seeing or hearing of some good that they are doing.

RECOGNIZE TRUTH

My people, the so-called Negroes, will soon learn and recognize the Truth for the author of Truth is with us. They yell their lungs out over a dead Prophet (Jesus of two thousand years ago), who cannot and did not come to do anything for us. He was not even sent to us but prophesied of ONE coming to us at the End of this World (the White Mans' World).

The White Race and their poison Bible (their slave-making Christianity) have poisoned the very hearts of my people against themselves and their God. One cannot unite the so-called Negroes in America without the help of Allah (God), for they care not for self-unity. They want love and unity with their enemies whom Allah (God) will destroy from the Face of the Earth in the very near future.

They are saying to me that if Allah does not want the enemies, they do not want Allah (God) nor a religion in which the White Race is not accepted. They make fools of themselves over their love for the enemies in spite of the fact that the White Slave masters kept our fathers out of their religion, Christianity, for approximately three hundred years—as long as they were in servitude slavery.

Our fathers made fools of themselves and their children for accepting the fixed and poisoned White Man's religion and Bible. Now, today, the white slave masters are scared stiff from looking at the consequence coming to them for deceiving the black nation with their poisonous slavery religious teachings, that they go and sit with you in your church.

TRY TO CONVINCE YOU

They do not go to hear you preach and teach them of their own religion, but to deceive you into thinking that now, we all shall be God's people together; and that the church is the place for you, and that you should not believe in any other religion other than Christianity.

They try to convince you that the church is Jesus' house, where he has put his name and the "Gates of Hell shall not prevail against it," and remember what he said to Peter: "Upon this rock I build my church."

After the injection of such poison, the so-called Negroes are lulled off to sleep, with the death of the ignorant – "The Gates of Hell will not try prevailing against itself," but, the "Gates of Heaven" are now prevailing against the church and all that she stands for. And, the "Gates of Hell" will not prevail against the "Gates of Heaven." (Allah and Islam).

If Peters' only confession was necessary for Jesus to build the church, he should have been able, with twelve disciples, to have converted all of the Jews and destroyed their Temples, with the stone of Peter. But, he did not; for Jesus was not the Founder of the White Mans' religion and church any more than Moses or the former Prophets of Allah (God).

The Bible further says that Jesus said to Peter, "Flesh and blood did not reveal it to him." We never get Divine Truth unless it comes through flesh and blood, but really the flesh and blood that will not reveal truth is the devil (White Race). Such is fulfilled today.

Hurry and join onto your own kind. The time of this world is at hand.

FEBRUARY 15, 1958 - THE ISLAMIC WORLD

New York Amsterdam News

"And among men there is he who disputes about Allah without knowledge and follows every rebellious devil; and it is written down that whoever takes him for a friend, he shall lead him astray and conduct him to the chastisement of the burning fire." (Holy Qur'an 22: 3-4).

I feel a bit ashamed for the public to think that I am writing these articles for any personal dislike of Rev. Violenes, nor do I believe that he personally dislikes me; but he is only prompted by the devils to dispute the truth.

Through his attempts to dispute the truth, of Allah (God), as revealed and taught to me and those before me, I hope that by the help of Allah (God), Rev. Violenes will be brought into the "light of truth," and if not, that the truth make him a public disgrace; and, thus bring many into the knowledge of truth who read, see, and hear of his ignorance and disgrace—all caused by the prompting of the devils.

There are thousands, yea, millions, who believe as Rev. Violenes believes. But, Allah, to Whom all praise is due, has not given the truth to me that I should hide it or be afraid. But, that I should cast it against falsehood and break its head, and its power and grip upon my people.

DEVILS FOR FRIENDS

The so-called Negroes have taken the devils for their friends instead of their own kind. As a result, the devils have and are still leading them astray; and finally, will cause them to suffer "hell fire" with them.

I will not dare discredit one prophet of Allah, nor his scripture, to the favor of another as the Christians do. I have made it clear in my column, according to the Holy Qur'an and the Bible, how evil it is and how ignorant for us to bear witness with the devils on their charge of adultery to Allah (God), by getting a son out of wedlock by Mary.

The religious scholars of the world will agree with me that it is charging God with adultery, since Jesus was of flesh and blood and his birth was in every respect as all other human beings.

SOME QUESTIONS

According to the Christian teachings of God, He is not flesh and blood; and since He (God) is not flesh and blood, what Glory would He have in flesh and blood? How can one claim sonship of that which by nature he is not of?

If Jesus' flesh and blood was only a shield for his real self, why did he not discard it on his resurrection from death? If he did not bring such a body (flesh and blood) from heaven, why should he carry such a body to heaven where there were no flesh and blood bodies; nor even the Father had one.

Jesus would look very odd and probably would feel lonely, sitting with flesh and blood body in the midst of spirits who have not even forms, demanding food, drink and clothing. It is a sin for you to be so deceived and to have such a misunderstanding of the Scriptures.

I have asked Rev. Violenes some time ago to prove that Jesus' religion was Christianity; or to prove that it was other than Islam; or to prove that it was from God; or that it had its roots in the Universal order of God's creation; or that Jesus' religion was other than Moses and the other prophets. But, he has made no attempts to answer me. Now comes the question of the Ten Commandments.

Muhammad, like all the other prophets, did not dare speak evil of God's revelations granted to the former prophets; but rather the Holy Qur'an has verified the truth of all the prophets. It recognized all truth of value from other Scriptures with respect and honor. But, I fear that you lack the truth of the Ten Commandments.

We, the Muslims, believe in One God. (Why do you set up a son as His equal, of whom God did not mention to Moses and Israel of such)? We, the Muslims, do not make graven images or pictures the likeness of God and put them in the Mosque. (But Christians do). We do not use the name of Allah in vain (but Christians do).

We do not steal (but Christians do). We love the brotherhood of Islam and the life and property of our brothers are sacred with us. (Not so among the Christians). We live and do the law of God while you only say and do not. We will not kill a Muslim (but Christians kill each other daily).

The Ten Commandments do not make it clear to us who is our neighbor that we should love as thy self, while enemies can live next door to us or even in our house. Islam makes a distinction that the believer is the brother of a believer. Doubtless to say you have not read or studied the beautiful, unequaled teachings of the Holy Qur'an Sharrieff. Both Moses and Jesus' Scriptures have been tampered with in the Bible by the devils, whom you hope to please and not God and Jesus.

MARCH 1, 1958 - THE ISLAMIC WORLD

Prayer In Islam
New York Amsterdam News

This is something that I have been trying to get around to writing for a long time. This Prayer Service performed by the Believers (Muslims) is one of the most beautiful services ever performed. Of all the Prayer Services of non-Muslims, I have never seen or read of one to equal the Prayer Service of the Muslims. I hope the non-Muslim readers of my article will pass their criticism of it when I have completed it.

I thought it to be most important to teach my people – the lost members of the Great Nation of Islam, found in the most evil and wicked part of our Planet Earth – this Prayer Service. We were never taught the proper way to serve and worship Allah (God), the Most Merciful God of the universe.

The way the American so-called Negroes are taught to pray, and worship God is wrong; and is even an insult to God and the Righteous. They say their prayers, on most occasions, unclean – of which they never give a thought – and many times the prayer is said in an unclean place.

TO ALLAH

The Islamic Prayer Service demands the prayer to be clean internally and externally as well when doing service to Allah (God). The Muslims, in one of their prayers, declare to Allah that they worship Him in the best manner, in these words:

"O Allah, we beseech Thy help, and ask Thy protection and believe in Thee, and trust in Thee, and we laud Thee in the best manner, and we thank Thee; and we are not ungrateful to Thee, and we cast off and forsake him who disobeys Thee.

"O Allah, Thee do we serve, and to Thee do we pray and

make obeisance, and to Thee do we flee, and we are quick, and we hope for Thy mercy and we fear Thy chastisement; for surely Thy chastisement overtakes the disbelievers."

I just had to write the whole of this prayer because I greatly admire those words that make it. Anyone will be touched, whether a believer or disbeliever, to see or be in the Muslims' Congregational Prayer Service, to see their sincere devotion to our Maker.

PURIFIES HEART

Prayer is the out-pouring of the heart's sentiments. A devout supplication to Allah (God) and a reverential expression of the soul's sincerest desires before its Maker. Prayer, according to the Holy Qur'an, is the true means of that purification of the heart, which is the only way to commune with Allah (God). The Holy Qur'an says: "Recite that which has been revealed to you of the book and keep up prayer; surely prayer keeps (one) away from indecency and evil, and certainly the remembrance of Allah is the greatest force." (29:45)

Prayer is a means of moral elevation of man. Prayer degenerating into a mere ritual, into a lifeless and vapid ceremony performed with insincerity of heart, is not the prayer enjoined by Islam.

Such prayer is expressly denounced by the Holy Qur'an: "Woe to the praying ones who are unmindful of their prayers." (107:4,5). To a Muslim, his prayer is his spiritual diet, of which he partakes five times a day. (A couple of times during the night), Says: Muhammad Ali.

SCHOLARLY WORK

I do not believe Maulvi Muhammad Ali as being the promised Mahdi. But, along with others, his scholarly work is admired as given to us in the translation of the Holy Qur'an into English, with the beautiful outline of the Muslims' Prayer

Service in his preface of the book. Preparation for Prayer:

Before saying prayers, it is necessary to wash those exposed parts of the body: (1st) The hands are cleaned up to the wrists. (2nd) The mouth is cleansed by means of a toothbrush or simply with water. (3rd) The nose is cleansed with water. (4th) The face is washed.

(5th) The right arm is washed, and then the left arm; both are washed up to the elbows. (6th) The head is then wiped over with wet hands. (7th) The feet are then washed up to the ankles; the right foot first and the left foot after, that is if the feet have been exposed. If not, then pass your wet hands over your socks.

The feet should be washed at least once every 24 hours, regardless to their being inside of shoes or boots. A fresh washing of the hands should be given whenever a man has answered a call of nature or has been asleep. In cases of husband and wife, a total bath of the whole body is necessary.

Hurry and join onto your own kind. The Time of This World is at Hand.

MARCH 8, 1958 - THE ISLAMIC WORLD

False Charges Made Against Prophets
New York Amsterdam News

"And say: O my Lord, I seek refuge in Thee from the evil suggestions of the devils and I seek refuge in Thee, O my Lord from their presence." (Holy Qur'an 23:97, 98).

False charges made against Divine Prophets and mockery of them by their enemies and the disbelievers are as old as the histories of the Prophets. All true Prophets of Allah know this, and therefore are well aware of what they will meet from their enemies when they received their missions. Allah (God) has never sent a prophet in which He did not make known to him the histories of those who went before him, and that which will come to pass in his mission.

Therefore, Muhammad (may the peace and blessings of Allah be upon him) is told to bear patiently what they say (Holy Qur'an 38: 17) and reminds him of the evil things that disbelievers said about the Prophets of Allah (God) before him.

I am not surprised to hear any white man or woman speak evil of Allah's Prophets, for they are the real haters, persecutors and murderers of Allah's (God's) Prophets. (Matthew 23: 37, Mark 12:5, Luke 22:2).

The Holy Qur'an is full of charges against the evil infidels who were ever planning against the life of the prophets, and charges them with killing the prophets.

"And most certainly we gave Moses the Book and we sent Apostles after him one after another; and we gave Jesus, the son of Mary, clear arguments and strengthened him with the Holy Spirit, what, whenever then an Apostle came to you with that which your souls did not desire, you were insolent so you called some liars and some you killed." (Ch. 2:97).

GUILTY PARTY

The white race, to whom near all the Prophets were sent, is the guilty party of teaching and writing false things against the Prophets. Naturally, their slaves (the so-called Negroes) will say that which their masters teach them to say.

That is why the so-called Negroes in the Scriptures are called blind, deaf, dumb and dead; and must be resurrected because of their ignorance of truth, love of the enemy, and hatred of self and kind. Therefore, the Holy Qur'an says: "And they follow what the devils fabricated." (Ch. 2:102).

The evil things the enemies of Islam write against the Prophet Muhammad is the same that was said of those Prophets which the Christians claim to be the Prophets of God. In fact, the Bible says even worse things about the life of the Prophets. If you only will read the Bible, you would wonder how any Christian could speak evil of Muhammad.

MAKES MOCKERY

The so-called Negroes naturally desire to say everything that they think will please their masters, as you will see in the writings of my proud, mockery-making opponent, Mr. Violenes, whom his own followers should be ashamed of. There is only one God that would recognize such evil mockery, and that one is the devil.

He (Mr. Violenes) is not intelligent enough to confine his attack to the religious point of view, he instead is launching a personal attack. Of course, I want him to remain throughout so that my people (the so-called Negroes) can see just what type preachers they have been represented by. I will not resort to name-calling. The Holy Qur'an is against it, and I am a Muslim.

LOOK AT SUCCESS

They love to mention Prophet Muhammad as one loving

and marrying many wives, as though the Bible is clear of such charges made against Prophets. Let us look at the spiritual success of this much-hated Muhammad by Christians. Just six hundred years after Jesus, he (Muhammad) came and within his own lifetime converted Arabia to Islam. (Jesus never did covert Palestine).

He (Muhammad) set men upright to the practicing and doings of righteousness. (The Christians never have practiced righteousness and never will).

He set up a universal brotherhood that has continued to grow all over the earth; love, freedom, justice and equality; obedience to the God of heaven and earth, a belief in all his Prophets and their Scriptures; and respect for the brotherhood and woman of our Nation. He was born in the Holy City Mecca (where no infidel is allowed, and the city held sacred by all the Prophets of God).

Could such a man with such continued success throughout the World of Righteousness be called an evil one? (A devil). If he married 100 wives, it seems that God was with him to conquer his enemies, as David was; whom the Bible claims to have had many hundreds of wives and concubines. Yet, the Christians sing his praises, and he was like God in his own heart.

Hurry and join onto our own kind. The Time of This World is at Hand.

MARCH 15, 1958 - THE ISLAMIC WORLD

The Bible's Wicked and Filthy Charges Against the Righteous.
New York Amsterdam News

"They say you are only of those deluded: And you are naught but a mortal like ourselves, and we know you to be certainly of the liars." (Holy Qur'an 26: 183, 186)

The disbelievers in the Prophets of God are disbelievers in God, the sender of the Prophets, and they are the same today as they were yesterday. It is surprising to see those who call themselves the representatives of God being the worst enemies of the Prophets of God and are always the friends of the enemies of God.

Such representatives love to make fun of the worthy and true representatives of God without even knowledge. They are puffed up with pride. They seem to feel secure from the chastisement of Allah (God) which will bring them to disgrace and ruin in the very eyes of those whom they mocked and sought to disgrace.

It is a very dangerous thing to do, to make mockery of the Great Arabian Prophet Muhammad (may the peace and the blessings of Allah be upon him) and the Great Universal Religion, Islam, to the joy and happiness of the devils, who are his teachers. Those fellows (the preachers) are the worst enemies that we have. One would meet with far less insults in talking or teaching Islam to real devils than you would by approaching the dumb preachers. They are pitiful.

POISON

Reverend George C. Violenes seems to delight himself in charging Prophet Muhammad (may the peace and blessings of Allah be upon him) of near 1400 years ago with polygamy and slavery; because his enemies make this charge against him.

I studied the life and teachings of Muhammad (may the peace and blessings of Allah be upon him) at the Congressional Library, which was written by his enemies, and most of them called themselves missionaries (preachers). Many of them even tried to translate the Holy Qur'an into English, I summed them all up in one word: POISON. I would feel ashamed of myself as a Muslim using their poisonous sayings of that great man and the great religion, Islam as witness. I do not even mention or refer to anything they say.

The true history of Muhammad and Islam is far from what the infidels have written. But, as I have said time and again, the Black Christian preachers are the so-called Negroes' worst enemies; for they are the friends of the so-called Negroes enemies.

In the days of Noah and his preaching and warnings, according to the Bible and Holy Qur'an, he was mocked by his enemies until the day of their destruction. They (the enemies) wanted to make the people believe that Noah was either crazy or an outright liar. But when the flood came, who was proven to be the liar?

CHARGES

Let us begin with the charge of wives and concubines that the Bible makes against its Prophets. Abraham, the friend of God (James 2:23) is charged with having a concubine (Gen. 16:1) after Sarah seemed to have been barren. She agrees and allows her husband to get children by Hagar, and this Hagar is called a slave of Abraham.

Abraham's nephew, Lot, after being delivered from the destruction of Sodom and Gomorrah, celebrated his deliverance with drunkenness. While drunk, his two daughters took turns laying with their father for two nights and both had babies from their father, Lot. (Gen. 19:33, 34, 35). What charge could be worse than to charge the Prophet with being drunk and then getting children by his own two daughters?

Hurry and join onto your own kind. The Time of This World is At Hand.

APRIL 12, 1958 - THE ISLAMIC WORLD

New York Amsterdam News

Without Divine guidance through Divine Prophets, people go astray from Allah (God). But the people whom Prophets are raised among to teach and explain the word or scripture of Allah (God) and His Prophets to, are the ones destroyed; these same ones who have been blessed with Divine Prophets as guides.

I quote to you the prayer of Abraham and his son, Ishmael as recorded in the Holy Qur'an 2: 127-129, that Allah raised up an Apostle for the lost-found so-called Negroes in the last days; "And when Abraham and Ishmael raised the foundation of the house, (the Kaaba in Mecca to serve as a sign of the type of the lost members of a chosen people),

"Our Lord accept from us, surely Thou art The Hearing, The Knowing; our Lord, make us both submissive to Thee, raise from our offspring a Nation submitting to Thee, and show us our ways of devotion and turn to us mercifully. Surely, Thou art the oft-returning to mercy, The Merciful; our Lord, raise up in them an Apostle from among them who shall recite to them Thy communications and teach them the Book and the wisdom, and purify them; surely, Thou art The Mighty, The Wise."

The above prayer is direct and fitting to the lost-found so-called Negroes in America who have not had before today a Divine interpreter of Allah's (God's) word and scriptures pertaining to others sent by the prophets of old. The "book" mostly refers to the Torah and the gospel given to Musa (Moses) and Isa (Jesus) and to the Holy Qur'an. These scriptures the so-called Negroes do not understand.

MISTAKES

They only guess and have made mistakes in trying to teach in their misunderstanding, and will not submit to a Divine interpreter, even though being blessed that the Divine interpreter is raised from among them. What greater blessing could God give than to choose His last Messenger from among us?

The true knowledge of the Bible would change the present Christian World's belief, for there is no salvation in it for the white Christian World. The white race never did accept the Divine Prophets that were sent among them. They persecuted and killed them and took the word and scriptures of God brought by those Prophets and added in and took out the truth to suit themselves, after having knowledge of the truth.

But the poor slaves (the so-called Negroes) never had such grand gifts until today. Therefore, they should not follow the way of that race of devils who killed the prophets of God that were sent to them.

Up to this very moment, you are following in the footsteps of the enemies. As it is written (2:130): "And whoever forsakes the religion (Islam) of Abraham is but he who makes himself a fool"

The past histories and the destructions of those who had forsaken the religion (Islam) of Abraham is sufficient proof.

"Allah raised Prophets as bearers of good news and as warners, and He revealed with them the Book with truth, that it might judge between people in that in which they differed; and none but the very people who were given it differed about it after clear arguments had come to them, revolting among themselves." The Torah and the Injil (the gospel) were given to the white race.

LOST MEMBERS

They are the race that the lost members of the black Nation would be found among. They are the ones have referred to as differing about the truth of the Bible and revolting among themselves, dividing their religion into parties because they hated the real truth contained in the Book and altered it.

By so doing, Allah has caused them to lose the real knowledge of it in order to prepare for a Nation submitting to Him. Their erroneous doing should serve as a warning to us today that we should follow their way in disbelieving the truth (the Holy Qur'an) after it comes to us.

Let not the Muslims (believers in the truth) take the unbelievers for friends rather than believers.

Hurry and join onto your own kind. The Time of This World Is At Hand.

APRIL 26, 1958 - THE ISLAMIC WORLD

New York Amsterdam News

"Oh, my servants, there is no fear for you this day, nor shall you grieve." (Holy Qur'an 73:68)

The fear of displeasing the slave masters, who are the enemies, haters, and murderers of the lost-found members of the Tribe of Shabazz, (the so-called Negroes) is causing millions of the American Black People to suffer, and finally will suffer "hell fire" for this fear!

The aim of Islam, which is now being preached throughout America to the fearful so-called Negroes, is to remove their fear of the slave masters, which is the greatest hindrance to their salvation.

"This day" as referred to in the above verse (meaning in the time of the presence of Almighty Allah (God), among the lost-found members of His people, lost for four hundred years from their Native Land and People, is the end of the time of the white race.

This race of people were not created to live on our Planet forever; only for six thousand years.

They are the only people on our Planet whose time was limited.

MISCHIEF-MAKING

We can clearly see today why Allah (God) limited their time—because of their mischief-making and causing bloodshed. It is impossible to live among them in peace. They are the World's meddlers and snoopers!

They are not contented to live alone without "snooping" around and meddling in other people's affairs. Even though you divide the earth equally with them, they would want your part, or try to run your own business for you the way that they think best.

The so-called Negroes will never get rid of the fear of their slave masters as long as they believe in the white race's religion (Christianity), and follow the scared preachers and politicians. You should not fear today.

You will not fear if you would only believe in Allah, His religion Islam, and follow me! Islam is the religion of our salvation. (You will soon come to know). There is no future for you and your families here!

Hurry and join me onto your own kind. The time of this world is at hand.

JUNE 28, 1958 - THE ISLAMIC WORLD

New York Amsterdam News

I think that I have made it clear to you that if we look forward to serving or meeting God. He must be in the form of a man. The Christians' Bible bears me witness that God is a man of flesh and blood. The Bible predicts God's coming as a man (Luke 21:27; Matthew 24:30; Revelation 1:7, 14:13). There is much proof in the Bible to support my claim that God is man, that is if you want proof.

You have been taught so long that God is not a man, so you have become hardened against believing in anything other than what you have been taught. "Every eye shall see him" (Revelation 1:7).

No eye can see spirits. The above chapter says: "All kindreds of the earth shall wail (shall be sorry to see His coming) because of Him." Never was this so true as it is today.

The wicked world of the devils (White Race) today, actually does not want a God of Righteousness to set up a Government of Justice and Righteousness (or they love what they have—wickedness, sport and play. Therefore, they are sorry and angry (Revelation 12:12, 13).

The devils see His (Son of Man) hand at work, and they are so upset that they are even preparing for the destruction while thinking that they are preparing for the destruction of others. The devils have, and still are leading the people away from the true God (Allah) and His true religion, Islam.

They never wanted Islam for their religion because they cannot live the life of the righteous. And, they do not want the so-called Negroes to believe in it nor pray to Allah.

WHY? Because Allah will answer prayer; and believing in Him and His religion will not only get us universal friendship but will get divine aid and help against your enemies.

We need a God who will help us and answer our prayers when we call on Him; not an unknown God (a mystery God), not a dead crucified Jesus of two thousand years ago; but we must remember that to get something worthwhile, we must be willing to sacrifice all that we have.

CLEAR LANGUAGE

The prophecy of Jesus (Luke 21:12) of the sacrifice and trials to be made by the so-called Negroes could not be expressed in a more clearer language: "But before all these, they (the devils) shall lay their hands on you, and persecute you delivering you (the Muslims) up to the synagogues (churches) and into prisons, being brought before kings and rulers for my name's sake."

It refers to none other than the so-called Negroes who accept their own religion Islam, and a Divine name from Allah. We are the hated ones in your midst and are persecuted for no other reason except that we are Muslims, and under other charges such as our not joining on their side after Truth and Righteousness has come to us, and knowing God, face to face, as we know each other's faces.

Shall we go back to that which He has brought us out of? NO! As it is written: "Shall the throne of iniquity have fellowship with thee, which frameth mischief by a law? They gather themselves together against the soul of the righteous, and condemn the innocent blood (the so-called American Negroes) (Psalms 94:20, 21); and again, it teaches, "Can there be fellowship with light and darkness?"

Let the American so-called Negroes return to their Allah and His Religion or suffer what was poured upon Pharaoh and his people for his opposition against Moses, the Servant of Allah.

Hurry and join onto your own kind. The time of this World is at hand.

JULY 5, 1958 - THE ISLAMIC WORLD

New York Amsterdam News

If we have the true knowledge of these two Books (Bible and Holy Qur'an), we could agree on the truth of God, devil, religion and the people of Allah (God). We cannot say and prove that the Bible is all the word of Allah (God). The Bible is near two-thirds prophecy— (what some others say that God said).

It is originally referred to as the "Book" because I suppose of the compilation of the Book which contains the Books of many others on histories, predictions, stories of rulers, people and nations, poems, parables, rules and laws.

The First Book called "Genesis" consists of an attempt at describing the creation and the history of the Old World; and steps taken by God towards the formation of the theocracy. The Second Book called "Exodus" – the history of Israel's departure from Egypt; the giving of the law. The third Book called "Leviticus" contains ceremonial laws. The Fourth Book called "Numbers" – the census of the people; the story of the wanderings in the wilderness. The Last Book called the "Revelations" contains very interesting symbolic predictions.

The English translators of the Bible dedicated the Book to one of their Kings. (King James of England). The first half of the Book is often referred to as the Torah. The second half is called the Gospel or New Testament.

The first part is also called the Old Testament. The two (Torah and the Gospel) are referred to as the two scriptures or Books; and cannot be proven to be the true Original Scriptures as given to Moses and Jesus.

The land of the Book (Bible) according to James C. Muir, author of "His Truth Endureth" and "Business Men of the Bible," was the center of the Ancient World, Egypt, Babylonia and Assyria; topography—The Jordan; the Sea of Galilee; the Dead

Sea. In these areas, "Egypt and Palestine" the religion of Islam is dominate, and there are no signs that Islam will not always be the dominating religion in those lands where the ancient prophets received their Scriptures.

This alone should be enough for the so-called Negroes to know that they were deceived by the arch deceiver (white race) in regard to the right religion. (Christianity or Islam).

The Bible is called Holy, and the word of God. Some of you go too far in such belief. The Bible is not all Holy, nor is it all the word of God! I hope that you who believe that it is all the word of God and Holy will read my proofs as taken from the Bible, which show that it is not all Holy and the word of God.

The preachers of the Bible should know that it is not all Holy without being told or proven that it is not. But most of these preachers' mouths and tongues are controlled by the enemy of truth for the sake of certain privileges; just as the fake prophets of Baal and the magicians of Pharaoh wanted to please the enemies of God!

Hurry and join onto your own kind. The Time of This World is at Hand.

JULY 26, 1958 - THE ISLAMIC WORLD

New York Amsterdam News

"Corruption has appeared in the land and sea on account of what the hands of men have wrought, that He (Allah) may make them taste a part of that which they have done." (Holy Qur'an 30:41)

We cannot deny the fact that the Christian West is responsible for this universal corruption in the land and sea. From the same corruptions that their own hands have wrought will come their doom.

The Christians preach that which they do not do and cannot do. Such as: "Love thy neighbor." I have as yet to meet one that loved his neighbor as he did himself. "Thou shall not kill." I have as yet to meet such a Christian. They even fight against each other but yet represent themselves as World peacemakers—with what?

The great deceiver of the World will reap what he has sown. Have they not corrupted many people and Nations under the false disguise of good peaceful loving Christians? The Christian West is full of the worst crimes, practicing evils and indecencies to the fullest and seeking to practice them on other Nations as well.

Universal tempters, ever parading before the World their bold half-nude girls and women—they are before your eyes in almost everything regardless. Murder, gambling, robbery, drunkenness, drugs, adultery, lying—there is hardly any end to it!

Their land and seas are filled with deadly weapons of war; her islands of sea she has filled with her corruption. Now she is hated and despised by all Nations of the earth, for she is proud and boastful, and desires to rule all people according to her wishes.

Her religion (Christianity) is a curse to us (the Black Man) and is full of slavery teaching. They have poisoned the Bible with their adding in and out of the truth. Now her doom is now in sight. It is their own work.

They fill the sea with powerful deadly ships, parking them off shore of the homes of other Nations. They secure airbases on foreign soil to park deadly bomb-carrying planes within striking distances of those whom she thinks to be her enemies.

Is not this the easy way to make enemies? Is this the act of a real Christian, the follower of Jesus whom they preach came for the peace of mankind, and to teach the sheathing of the sword, and the turning of the other cheek? Where is a good Christian among this race?

LOVE MEDDLING

They love meddling in other people's affairs, they are in every fight or war, regardless to whom or where; yet crying "peace, peace" with every deadly modern weapon of war, brandishing them before the Nations as a dare. Shall not the God of Peace and Justice deal with such troublemaking people as He did to those before you of old?

I warn every one of you my people fly to Allah and follow me! As I warned you in New York on the 6th of this month, the judgment of this world has arrived! Get out of the Church and get into the Mosques, and join onto your own kind, the Nation of Islam! The house you are in shall surely fall and never rise again!

I shall see you on the 3rd of August in Pittsburgh, Pennsylvania, if Allah's Will.

Hurry and join onto your own kind. The Time of This World is at Hand.

AUGUST 2, 1958 - THE ISLAMIC WORLD

WE MUST HAVE SOME EARTH
New York Amsterdam News

What good is it to serve a Master or God if that Master or God will not give you a home on His earth that you can call your own? There are 57,255,000 square miles of land out of water. Of a total 196,940,000 square miles that make up our planet, and 29,000,000 square miles of producing land, how many square miles of this good earth do we, the so-called American Negroes, own here in America?

Yet, we seek to be recognized as the equal of our slave master's children with nothing but a job that the masters allow us to do for them when we are wanted. Is not this a shame for us whom the slave masters claimed that they freed nearly one hundred years ago to go for our own selves?

We have never tried going for self. The white man drives us and forces us to do something for himself and his kin, and yet we have made ourselves appear to the World of Mankind to be the laziest cowards, self-divided, shameful, disgraceful beggars of white people on the earth!

Do not we ever get tired of being looked upon as fools without a home? Everyone has some of this earth that they call their own (if not, they are doing everything within their power to own some of it.)

For the past one hundred years of freedom (so-called), we have given the same slave masters our labor and our lives to help build them a home and keep it secure for them; though the white slave masters are responsible for our blindness— (but not after the light comes to us).

SATISFIED WITH NOTHING

We need re-education! The white man education is helpful, but there is not enough light shown in it for the so-called Negroes to find the way to self. They beat and kill you, starve you, drive and kick you out of their presence and homes; yet you love and admire them, and hate and dislike yourselves, and will not unite to find a home for self and children. You are a satisfied people with nothing!

We must have some of this earth that we can call our own! We have lost 400 years making our slave master's children rich, powerful, and independent, and are charmed by their riches (as the symbolic parable of Lazarus and the rich man) in that you will not go after something for self!

No. 1—We are where we do not belong, and by the Divine Prophet's prophecy concerning us, there is no permanent home for us in this part of our planet; but promised us a permanent home among our own people. Would not you like to live in peace and be recognized and treated as brother citizens by your own people in your own country than to be unrecognized and treated like a "dog" by other than your own kind and country?

PERMANENT HOME

Allah (God) wants to give you, the so-called Negroes, the best and most permanent home the earth has to offer. The white man came into possession of this part of our planet by blood and built by blood and established himself by evil (Hab. 2:12) and now must pay the price set by Allah (God) through the mouth of His prophets.

We must have some of this earth that we can call our own for a permanent home. Come, follow me, and you will get it. For this cause is the base of Allah's (God's) coming! Do not let this world of our enemies deceive you!

Allah (God) wants to give you, the so-called Negroes, the best and most permanent home the earth has to offer. The white man came into possession of this part of our planet by blood and built up blood and established himself by evil (Habakkuk 2:12), and now must pay the price set by Allah (God) through the mouth of his prophets. We must have some of this earth that we can call our own for a permanent home. Come, follow me and you will get it, for this cause is the base of Allah's (God's) coming. Do not let this world of our enemies deceive you.

Hurry and join onto your own kind. The time of this world is at hand.

RARE ARTICLES SECTION

This section is composed of Articles from the Los Angeles Herald Dispatch and the Chicago New Crusader. Due to the fact that most of the old "Negro Press" publications are non-extant and due to inadequate preservation processes this section is without specific dates but falls within the general time period of years 1957-1962. Prior to the publication of the Muhammad Speaks Newspaper in October 1961 and its immediate predecessor Mr. Muhammad Speaks, the Nation of Islam utilized several newspapers from the "Negro Press" to help to distribute the message of the Most Honorable Elijah Muhammad. These historic news organs include: The Pittsburgh Courier, The New York Amsterdam News, The Los Angeles Herald Dispatch, The Westchester Observer, The New Jersey Herald News and the Chicago New Crusader. Volume 3 of the Invincible Truth Series will feature the 3 years of the Most Honorable Elijah Muhammad's articles published in the Westchester Observer.

A NATION IN A NATION

We, the once slaves, have grown to be a nation of twenty million or more in a nation that enslaved our fathers, and to this day has deprived us of equal justice under their own laws. We have no equal civil right – most of us are treated by white citizens of America as animals. It is common to see and hear of white mobs attacking, beating and shooting down poor blacks, whose fathers and mothers labor, sweat and blood helped make America the richest government on earth; nevertheless, we are yet the most hated and mistreated people.

Allah (God) wants to make a great nation out of us (so-called Negroes). But if we desire to remain the slave or servants for our slave masters, it is all right with Allah. Do we love ourselves and our children? If so, why not we build a future for ourselves rather than beg the same slave masters for jobs, and equal shares in whatever they have – even to equal membership in their society and families (inter-marriage).

This is definitely not a wise thing to do, but a very foolish and destructive thing for the once slave and his master to do. By the help and guidance of Allah (God), I have put before you the wise and best thing for your future.

Firstly, some of this earth that we can call our own. Without some of this earth that we can call our own, we cannot hope to even become a free nation out of the nation of the slave master. IT IS FAR MORE IMPORTANT TO TEACH SEPARATION OF THE BLACKS AND WHITES IN AMERICA THAN PRAYER. Teach and train the blacks to do something for self in the way of uniting and seeking a home on this earth that they can call their own!

There is no such thing as living in peace with white Americans. You and I have tried without success. Look what white Americans did to my followers in Los Angeles, California on April 27, 1962. They know that we, the Muslims, are a peaceful people and do not carry arms, but the heartless, enemy devils care not for peace, they were created and made to hate peace. Night and day, they are out seeking a chance to beat and kill you, while at the same time you are out seeking to show them HOW MUCH YOU LOVE THEM. A very foolish people you are. How can anyone other than you (so-called Negroes) love and open enemy?

It is the right time that we have INDEPENDENCE for our nation from the evils of our open enemies, and not the foolish things other organizations are doing. They want our people integrated into our open enemies, to be destroyed as a people. They seek that recognition, which demands better qualifications; education, knowledge of self and others, manners and self-respect and the respect of others. But our people just do not have these qualifications until they first come to Islam and bear witness to what Allah (God) has revealed to me. No intelligent and refined society will accept us until we have the above stated qualifications.

We just cannot compete with them in business unless we unite and get some of this earth that we can produce our own people needs. For example, here in Chicago, Illinois, the black man is robbed on the Southside of the city through giant cut rate stores owned by the white man, who makes it almost impossible for black peoples independent stores to survive. But with the right understanding and business unity among us, we could turn this great flow of millions of dollars from going to the Northside's White businessmen back into the pockets of the poor Blackman on the Southside. ASK ME HOW YOU CAN DO IT?

We must stop being foolish as to spend our few hard-earned dollars with the rich of the land. You who are wealthy or rich among us should help set up independent businesses that your people demand which would add wealth to your people and also yourself through lower prices. This would also give employment to our people. But to be successful, WE MUST HAVE SOME OF THIS EARTH TO PRODUCE OUR PEOPLES

NEEDS.

HURRY AND JOIN ONTO YOUR OWN KIND. THE TIME OF THIS WORLD IS AT HAND.

A UNITED BLACK NATION

WHY NOT A UNITED TWENTY MILLION BLACK PEOPLE OF AMERICA? There is a United Nations, headed by America and England, which includes nearly all races and colors. There is also a United Arab Republic.

Twenty million Black people of America are called after the names of their slave-masters. This means that they are still the property of White America; thus, making it impossible for them to become a free and independent people of White America. If they (the so-called Negroes) would unite and throw off the White man's names—which have no divine meanings, for they (the devils are not the people of the God of righteousness (Isaiah 63:19; 64:3-5)—and the slavery teachings of the White man's religion (Christianity), they, in the Name of Allah and the religion Islam, could become one of the greatest and mightiest nations on the earth. (Let the **disbelievers ask me to prove it).**

We must unite and qualify for self-independence, for Allah's earth is vast. America killed off the original owners (the Indians) and took this country for their home. We must have some of this earth that we can call OUR OWN. Allah is with us. We must learn trades and professions of all kinds and build our own nation, which consists of twenty million so-called Negroes.

There is no hope of a future for us in the White race, because they have no future for themselves. **THIS YOU MUST KNOW!** Unity is the result of love and respect of one's own and others. We cannot expect love, unity and respect from others until we have these for ourselves. We should be ashamed of ourselves to ever want to integrate or mix bloods with the very enemies and murderers of our people. They are born haters and despisers of the Black nation, they are also the robbers and spoilers of our nation.

Why not a unified American Black people (the so-called Negroes)? We have a world of people of our kind who would not hesitate to show us that they are our sincere brothers and sisters if we only would throw off the chains and yoke of the White man's slavery. You should drop their names and get out of their religion. Stop worshipping them (White man) and worship Allah (God) and His true religion, Islam. Islam means entire submission to the will of Allah and the entrance into His peace; there you will not fear nor shall you grieve.

Seek for yourself and kind, that which the White race seeks for themselves which is independence, freedom, justice, equality and a free country for their own kind. A dependent and begging people cannot hope for anything but the worst. This world is on her way out and another one is coming in, the new world of Islam (Peace and Righteousness) under the rulership of Allah and the Muslims.

Let us buy farm land where we can grow our food and sell it at a price that our poor people are able to pay. We should produce our own needs, unite as one man, and sacrifice everything to accomplish this unity.

HURRY AND JOIN ONTO YOUR OWN KIND. THE TIME OF THIS WORLD IS AT HAND.

A UNITED BLACK NATION II

This is a great time of national and international disagreement because of the united Black African and Asian nations. The leaders that are presently heading the Asian and African countries are not seeking self-glory and prestige, but are rather seeking freedom, justice and equality and self-government to represent the voice and carry out the will of their people.

Great historical strides are being taken to revolutionize the economic, political, social and educational systems of these countries. They are tired of foreign domination and rule by other than their own kind. They want to do business with their own nation. They desire to hold conferences of good will and diplomacy with others like themselves. They have experienced the painful error of doing business with their oppressors (the White man). You see our people of other lands putting forth every united effort to restore love, peace and happiness among their own kind.

When we look at our own darker people in Africa, the picture of love and unity does not exist. We are so disunited in our purpose and aim that it may appear, at first, hopeless to solve our problem. We find a situation in America, worse than it was in Egypt when the Israelites were in bondage to the Egyptians. In those days, God, through His Mercy, raised from among the common people, a leader who was living in poverty, who was illiterate and uneducated.

Therefore, when God (Jehovah) called Moses to unite his people, and lead them forth, out of the land of the Egyptians, many of the Israelites, for whom Moses was raised up, opposed him. Today, you think of Moses as a great leader of his people. You also bestow the same honor upon Jeremiah, David, Solomon, Lot and the others. You read in their histories where they were rejected, hated and despised by their own people more than by the enemy of their people.

It is recorded that when Moses inquired of Jehovah what he should say to Pharaoh and to the people, God told him that He would put into the mouth of Moses the proper words, for He, Jehovah, made Moses' mouth and tongue and made Moses His mouthpiece to the people. From the Holy Qur'an, I here verify the Words of God to me, where He says: "And I have possession of Power over all things!" I say to you none other than what Allah has permitted me to say to you. He alone is my guide and my speech: His Will is my will! I say to you, unite and separate from the people of this modern house of bondage.

To this Modern Pharaoh I say, "Let my people go!" The so-called Negro Leaders who are blind to the time, do not realize that this is the time of our separation, and that God is dealing with America today as He dealt with Egypt and the nations in the past. Therefore, it is fruitless for a man, who has not received his instructions from God to bring about the desired peace and prosperity of our people. He cannot successfully represent this people. No self-made or self-styled leader, whose authority is NOT from God Himself, can do this job.

If we bring Moses' history right down front to modern times, we will gain a better understanding of the time. It was the magicians, the officials and the various leaders in Moses' day who opposed him most severely, because they loved the honor of Pharaoh more than Jehovah and their own people. They did not want to bow to a man who was uneducated according to their standards of values, which were really the standards of values of the enemy of their people.

Is this not equally true today of the so-called Negro intellectual class, because of their pride, self-conceit and ambition, they cannot submit to Divine Leadership, one not educated according to their standards, which are really the standards of the **White man (the enemy of God and themselves)?**

Muhammad of 1400 years ago, was also a man of no

education and was severely opposed by the same kind of intelligencia leadership that exists in the ways of the world. The university-trained man is often too proud and boastful of his education and will not sincerely cater to the welfare of his people. These are the very same reasons why Jesus was not able to win converts and followers from among the highly educated and rich people in is day. They recognized the enemy as their God, as you recognize the White man (enemy) as your God today.

Let us consider that it is in the deep soil deposits of the earth where precious stones and jewels are discovered. It is among the poorer class of people where great artists, writers and leaders are found, not from among the rich and wealthy class of people. Such ones found in the mud of civilization have a better knowledge and understanding of the needs of the majority of their people. What you need, is what God Himself desires for us to have, and that is a united Black leadership in North America, with one shepherd over His flock. Whether you accept the religion of Peace (Islam) or not, it is my desire, by the Help of Almighty God, to feed the mouths of the hungry, to shelter the homeless, to clothe the naked, to provide every need that is necessary for the development of an advanced Black leadership for my people, anywhere you choose to go on this planet earth.

Be it here in America, Africa or Asia: in the Desert Regions of the Sahara, Arabian Desert or in the desert regions of America's southwest, God has the Power, which is on our side today, to bring forth vegetation and foliage growth, gardens and heaven for you and me, even if it is the desert and swamp lands of the earth!

HURRY AND JOIN UNTO YOUR OWN KIND. THE TIME OF THIS WORLD IS AT HAND.

ALLAH SAYS: ACCEPT YOUR OWN

The acceptance of one's own is justified by the law of justice as an act of self-pride and intelligence. If we object to the acceptance of our own, whose own can we accept without being classified as fools without self-pride? Self comes first by all civilized people.

What is our own? Spiritually, Allah answers that: we are the righteous and were made other than righteous by the devils who enslaved us and robbed us of the knowledge of self and our own. If Allah (God) has numbered us as being members of the righteous nation, the original, the first people in the Sun, then our OWN includes everything in the Sun.

LOST AND FOUND PEOPLE

The whole of the universe. We are recognized throughout Asia and Africa today, as being their lost and found people. Mr. Lomax learned this on his recent visit to Africa seeking the inside story of his people for his slave masters. Most so-called Negro journalists are only the devil's informers of the secrets of the Black man!

The Asiatic and the African are now closing their doors against all so-called American Negroes, except those who confess Islam—the Muslims.

The Negro leadership, both religious and political, because of their love for the White race, White Christianity and their hatred of the Black nation and their religion Islam (the true religion of God), are rejected by the Islamic world which includes Asia and Africa.

MADE TO SERVE ENEMY

We must agree on common sense, that we were brought here by our enemies (the White race) and made to serve them. We are the product of our enemies' own makings. Whatever we are today, it is the work of our enemies (the White race).

Today, they despise and hate us, the product of their own making! They scorn, make mockery of our laziness, ignorance, filthiness, drunkenness and our hatred of each other!

Since the Black man of Africa and Asia are not such people as we are, then who is to blame? They (White race) spent 400 years in making the so-called Negroes what they are today.

Allah (God) desires to make us a people for Himself and if we submit to Him, He will give us back our **OWN**, (the mastery of the Universe). We cannot exist further under other than our OWN, for there will not exist other than our own, after this great, final war between Allah and the devils.

HEIGHT OF IGNORANCE

The desire and want of the Black man and woman of America to mix blood with the devils is the height of ignorance! Nearly 90% of the so-called Negroes would forgive the devils for the evils done to their parents and selves today, if the devils only accept them as his own. Even the preachers, who should know that there is no such thing as a forgiving of the devils by Allah (God), preach that their people should love the devils and forget the past! Allah cannot forgive the devils and keep his promise to the prophets, that He would destroy Satan, the devil, who had deceived the nations of the earth. Allah cannot forgive the devils and keep his promise to the prophets, that He would destroy Satan, the devil, who had deceived the nations of the earth. Why not accept your OWN? You are the best, the most beautiful, the most powerful, the FIRST and the LAST! Love your OWN and keep your OWN!

ALLAH COMES FROM HEAVEN INTO HELL

Since the coming of our Saviour, the Mahdi, the One Spoken of in the religious scriptures of the past as the Son of Man, and the Messiah, who came in the Person of Master Fard Muhammad, many great and wonderful events have taken place among our people (so called Negroes of America). The majority of my people have not realized the blessings we are receiving or the great love that Almighty Allah has for us. There is none who loves us to the equal of our Savior, Master Fard Muhammad (God in Person). He, Alone, came into this part of the earth filled with all manner of evil and corruption to teach us the ways of righteousness. For this is the land (America) that is like unto ancient Babylon which was destroyed because of her sins and corruption.

ALLAH COMES FROM HEAVEN INTO HELL

He (Allah) came out of Heaven into Hell (North America) to save us from destruction that is hovering above this nation. America's inescapable and timely end is set as in the rising and setting of the sun. As I have made clear in my last two articles, we, of all people and of people of all nations did not know who we were before the Coming of Allah, therefore, we have been open prey to our enemies (White Race). In fact, all nations of the earth have taken advantage of the poor Black man and woman in the mud in this part of the earth.

Though our first parents brought to this country were not ignorant to the knowledge of themselves, they were soon either killed by the white slave masters or died from grief. The slave masters then subjected our fore-parents children to their filthy lust and wicked deceiving teachings. Thus, we have been reared today from the soil of corruption and from the seed of their hate, murder violence and blood. It is not easy to separate you from their evil influence and practices when you believe all the lies the slave masters taught us ABOUT OURSELVES during these past 400 years.

LOST AND FOUND NATION OF ISLAM

We (so called Negroes) have been named the Lost and Found Nation of Islam, a name or title given to us by the religious scientist of the East to describe so-called Negroes of America who would be lost for over 400 years, and who in the last days of this present world would be found wandering blindly in a strange land like helpless lambs in the midst of ravaging wolves. If you are yet in doubt as to the truth of this history, I ask you to name another people who have been lost from their native land are presently living in a foreign land with no desire to return home because the enemy, who captured them has killed within them a desire to reclaim their own. Name another people, who do not know their native tongue and speak only the master's language. What other people, besides so-called Negroes, have the religion and history of that people been so concealed and hidden, leaving no possible chance for this knowledge to escape, except by the Will and Power of God, Himself? There are no other people who fit this description but the so-called American Negroes.

HURRY and JOIN onto YOUR OWN KIND. THE TIME OF THIS WORLD IS AT HAND.

ALLAH OFFERS YOU A FUTURE

You and I, the so-called American Negroes, are helpless without Allah (God) and Islam, which is the religion of God, His Prophets and our people. We are at the mercy of the Christian World. What has the Christian World done for you and me? Why should we want to remain in it? Have not they continued to segregate you, line you up and burn you, don't they continue to beat your heads and your brains burst out over your ears and eyes? They have done these things to us. They did these things even as you called yourself a Christian. They have shown that they don't want you as a brother. They have shown they don't recognize you as their equal. Why don't you exercise that freedom which they offer you and go back to your own?

If our share of this earth is not in this Western Hemisphere, then we must look for it in the East. However, 25,000,000 so-called Negroes who have been lost from their own people for 400 years must have a home on this earth that they can call their own. Allah the Great God of the universe will give us the whole earth if we submit to Him and have patience to wait on Him. Regardless of the cost, we must have some earth of our own. Let not the false show and promises of this world deceive you so that you be the loser.

You make yourself a despised people in the eyes of the civilized world by hating yourself and loving the enemy (devil). The Original man, Allah has declared, is none other than the Black man. He is the first and last, maker and owner of the Universe. The brown, yellow, red and white all come from the Black man. The Black man used a special method of birth control law to produce the White race.

The true knowledge of Black and White mankind should be enough to awaken the so-called Negroes, put them on their feet and on the road to self-independence. You, my people, are so afraid of the slave-master, that you even love them to the point of your own destruction. You wish the bearer of truth would not tell the truth even if he knows it. You hate a leader that tries to unite you to your own kind.

Allah offers you a future, an eternal future. This world has no future. It was doomed when it was created. I speak and write what has been given to me from Allah (God) to whom praise is due. I am not here to excite you for wealth or praise. I don't want your wealth. I don't want your praise. I want for you the thing which will produce unity of self and our kind. I want you safe. The world knows that I want you safe. What I preach is for our own life and the life of our children.

It is Allah's will and purpose that we shall know ourselves. He came Himself to teach us the knowledge of self. How else may you account for the success of my followers and myself? Who is better knowing of who we are than God Himself? All praise is due to the Great Mahdi (Allah in Person), Who was to come and has come. He is the Sole Master of the Worlds. I ask myself at times, "What can I do to repay Allah (the Great Mahdi, Fard Muhammad) for His coming, wisdom, knowledge and understanding?"

My followers and I have and are still spending much time and money to awaken our people to the knowledge of self. We are suffering much persecution and ridicule to awaken our people to the knowledge of their own salvation. Our present suffering is nothing compared to the joy that awaits us as a people united for one common cause serving Allah, The God of Abraham, Moses, Jesus and our forefathers. Allah has declared that we must know ourselves and unite to our own kind or suffer the consequences. The new government controlled by the Roman Catholics will stop at nothing in their effort to win the Black people of America to them, but the Negroes must know that this world's end is near.

HURRY AND JOIN ONTO YOUR OWN KIND. THE TIME OF THIS WORLD IS AT HAND.

AMERICA PERSECUTES THE MUSLIMS

The Monroe, Louisiana, city police made a wanton, lawless, brutal, beastly attack on the peaceful, religious meeting of my followers Sunday, March 5, 1961. Then these law-breaking police officers placed false charges on my followers to cover up their law-breaking crimes and complete disregard of protection provisions in the United States Constitution.

My people, the so-called American Negroes, have long been the victims of attacks by their slave-masters. The enemy always go free after doing these unjust things to our people. The history and record is filled with the facts of how the slave-master fails to bring his own to trial for breaking their own laws in mistreating us and denying us justice.

America tells the Negro he is an equal citizen and must fight for America, but America denies him justice. The so-called Negro has been declared an equal citizen. Where is this equal citizenship? It is only in words! It has not been in deeds! The so-called Negro does not have freedom in liberties of government that the slave-master enjoys, yet, America refers to him as a citizen on an equal basis with the slave-master. The U.S. Constitution declares equal justice for all. This equal justice is never practiced on the so-called Negro. Since America cannot follow their own laws of the country, not to mention the laws of nature, why not separate the so-called Negro? By so doing, American would not be charged with injustice to her former slave. The so-called Negro in America has never had the opportunity to go for self.

If the slave-master said to his slave 100 years ago, "You are free," why didn't the slave-master send the so-called Negro back to where he came from, on his own land? Then say to his people: "Here is your brother that we kidnapped three hundred and ten years ago." No! The slave-master kept him caged in. If you take a wild bird and cage him, you are responsible for his well-being, treatment and protection—but no, you killed and burned the bird. If you let the bird out of the cage, giving him the opportunity to return among his own flock, the bird is then free to fly where it pleases.

The so-called Negro is here in your midst as you kidnapped and brought him here more than 400 years ago. You have now set up an invisible chain and an invisible wall of limitations about him.

Under your religious and political system, you are always promising him that you will do better. You never do! Since you can't follow your own laws of justice and protection towards your servant, the so-called Negro, let him go! You then can represent America as a place of equal justice for all or separate them here into a place to themselves. Let them live in peace and God will let you live in peace.

It was terrible the way Police Chief Kelly of Monroe broke and forced his way into a peaceful assembly of people gathered to worship Allah, the God of their forefathers, the prophets and of their choosing. He even warned some of the followers the night before that he would break up their meeting if they attempted to hold a religious service devoted to the religion of Islam.

The Monroe police, armed with weapons, broke down the doors to the Mosque. They broke in on unarmed people with heavy Billie clubs, brass knuckles and drawn pistols. Among the people gathered to worship were women and children with the wife of the minister present, who is four months pregnant. The police started beating on them. The police in beating, did not use ordinary police sticks, but the big heavy sticks similar to the kind their ancestors used in the caves and hillsides of Europe to guard themselves at night against attacks by beasts.

This Police Chief Kelly, then in court says (and it is in the record to be examined if they have not tried to cover it up, too!) that he went to Muhammad's Mosque religious service because he had a suspicion that this religion was subversive from what he had read and heard! Yet he did not place this charge of subversion against my followers to bring them to court! If we are subversive and are trying to overthrow the government of America by force, let him or any other who say so, carry us into the Federal courts of justice and prove it!

Are not Police Chief Kelly and Judge W. M. Harper acquainted with the provision of the United States Constitution which states there shall be no law respecting an establishment of religion, or prohibiting the free exercise thereof, or abridging the freedom of speech; or the right of the people peaceably to assemble? Is this provision only meant to apply to White people? Why continue to persecute my followers under Police Chief Kelly's false charges?

If there was ever a time that we should be united regardless of religious beliefs, it is now! Why can't we unite? Is it not due to fear of not pleasing the slave-masters? WE must build a future for our children. Not the future that the White race has built for us, which is nothing but slavery, begging, suffering, injustice, disgrace, and murder at their hands. The Negro leadership should take examples from our people in Africa and Asia, who also were deceived, robbed, and enslaved by the White race of Europe and America, under the White man's slavery teachings of Christianity. Now, Africa and Asia have awakened to the knowledge of their deceivers and are throwing them and their damnable teaching out. Africa and Asia are now returning to the true religion of God (Allah), the same as I am teaching here and have been for 30 years, and they are on the road to success.

Why do you feel proud now over what belongs to the White man? You own nothing here but the freedom to be a fool for White America. The college-trained Negro clergy, politician and educator knows that there is no future for them under White Christianity. They have neither a country, nor a chance to build a civilization for their own people yet they refuse to take part with me in the sure program of God for our people—even after watching our success daily. Soon we will strip them of their followers and then we will see if their beloved White friends will be their followers, whom they now are greatly admiring to the destruction of their own people who are now in the mud. Why shouldn't you and I work together for the common good of our people in America?

Hurry to join onto your own kind. The time of this world is at hand.

AMERICANS PERSECUTE THE MUSLIMS, WHAT WILL BE HER END?

(Continued from previous article)

"And they cried with a loud voice, saying, How long O Lord, Holy and true, dost thou not judge and avenge our blood on them that dwell on the earth?"

The above verse is a prophecy of the lost and found people of the Black Nation of Islam called "Negroes" by their enemies (the American White devils) who have persecuted and killed Black people for the past 400 years. Some think this verse might refer to some of the Muslims who came here some years ago and were persecuted by these same devils and are now in jails here in the U.S.A. Some of them have been held here in prison some 40 years so Allah (God) told. They also were persecuted for trying to teach our people here in America the true religion, called Islam.

It can be understood clearly in these words: "How long O Lord, Holy and true, does Thou not judge and avenge our blood on them that dwell on the earth? We all dwell on the earth, but why the "earth" is really used here (in this verse) is to distinguish between the place where this enemy dwells and the place or country of the Muslims, called the Holy Land. Europe and America used to be called the wilderness or home of the exile demons.

The so-called Negroes are the only people whose history shows have been beaten and killed daily by another people, for the past 400 years. The jails of America are now filled with the poor so-called Negroes mixed with the Muslims. The so-called Negro prisoners are fast becoming converts to Islam. This is Allah's (God's) doings that the scripture may be fulfilled; wherein it says: "which executeth Judgment for the oppressed: which giveth food to the hungry. The Lord looseth the prisoners." (Psalms 146:7; Acts 12L 17; Revelation 2:10).

The Government of America hates her slaves (so-called Negroes) more than any of her outside enemies. She treats the so-called Negroes as if they were enemies of hers, who once made them prisoners and ruled them under a very wicked hand, whom the Americans finally overcame and now takes revenge on her oppressors for their past evils done to the people of America. The poor so-called Negroes have never been able to get along with their masters (White race) in peace. This proves to the so-called Negroes that Allah's word is true.

"Twelve Leaders" from all over the Planet had a conference in the Holy City Mecca, Arabia, over the Lost-Found Nation (the so-called Negroes) in the wilderness (America) who must return to their own. These leaders agreed that the devils (the American White race) are disagreeable to live with in peace and have decided to remove them from the Planet Earth. I will agree with the scientists, for we have tried to live with them in peace, even up to this very minute (400 years) and they yet show the world that they do not want any peace with any Black people.

Let us read another prophesy of America's cruel treatment of the so-called Negroes under Allah's deliverance of the enslaved so-called Negroes from her hands in these words: "He who smote the people in wrath with a continual stroke, he that ruled the Nations in anger, is persecuted, and none hindereth." "That made the whole earth as a wilderness and destroyed the cities thereof; that opened not the house of his prisoners." (Isaiah 14:6, 17)

Another true prophecy made by Jesus of the persecution of the Muslims: "But take heed to yourselves, for they shall deliver you up to councils; and in the synagogues ye shall be beaten, and you shall be brought before rulers and kings for my sake, for a testimony against them." (Mark 13:9). All so-called Negroes who accept the truth (Islam) may expect such persecution and be hated for accepting the Name of Allah or one of the ninety-nine attributes of Allah. "Muhammad" or Mohammed" is a Name of Allah (God), which means praise and one who is worth of praise and is praised much. These are the names prophesied in the Bible: (Chronicles 7:14; Isaiah 43:7; 40:26). America would like to frighten the Black people away from their salvation in Islam, by persecuting the Believers.

Allah makes the Muslims fearless and will soon put fear and trembling in the hearts of our enemies. Allah will bring upon America that which He has never brought upon people in the past and never will be the like of such judgment anymore. America must pay for her evils done to us. There is no such thing as forgiving! Allah said to me that He would repay her for all that she has and is doing against us.

HURRY AND JOIN ONTO YOUR OWN KIND! THE TIME OF THIS WORLD IS AT HAND!

AMERICA WILL DESTROY HERSELF

"For thou hast said in thine heart, I will ascend into Heaven, I will exalt my throne above the Stars of God (this throne represents a false religion, opposing the true religion); I will sit also upon the mount of the congregation in the sides of the North." Isaiah 14:13.

INTERPRETATION

Here Satan, the devil makes an attempt to equal himself with Allah (Jehovah) who created the heavens and the earth; Satan had no part in the creation of the heavens and the earth, therefore, cannot ever be the equal of Allah, in power. But in his heart, he secretly believes that he can with his newly acquired knowledge of gravitation and the power of the atoms.

Satan believes that he has conquered water, land, air. Now, he seeks to conquer the space to get out of the confines of the gravitation of earth and he thinks he will be independent to the power of Allah to destroy him, and to be Allah's equal in power over life on the earth.

SATAN EXALTS HIMSELF

He makes or exalts himself above the very chief scientists (the Stars of God) of Allah's in wisdom; he seeks to establish and mount his religion and followers above the true religion and followers of Allah (God).

He will sit upon the mount of the congregation (make himself like God over the people; the vice-gerent of God) in the sides of the North. Not in the East (the Holy City of Mecca) where the congregation of Allah assembles – the Muslims.

It is the religion of Christianity with its head in Rome called the Pope or Father of the Christian Church, who has tried to set organized Christianity above the true religion of Allah

(Islam) and to turn the people from the spiritual center of Allah's Mecca, Arabia.

HAD ARMY OF ELEPHANTS

The Pope tried to do this even by war in the year 570 A.D. with Abraha, the Emperor of Ethiopia, with an army mounted on elephants. As history shows, this was a miserable failure. They may, according to the Bible (Revelation 20:9) attempt to attack the Holy City Mecca again by air at their final end, but that too will be a failure.

The religious history of Rome shows many false Gods at its head. She is backed by the wealth and might of the white race. (See Revelation 17:1-7.) Mecca is backed also by wealth and power, but of Allah and the Nation of Islam for which every Muslim on the Planet Earth would die before they would allow any nation or nations to attack and destroy the city.

The devils have always desired to be the rulers of the people of God. This is the nature in which they were created (grafted). The devils were given the power to rule the righteous people of the earth for six thousand years. Now, that time is up! But they desire to remain the rulers of the people. This desire cannot be removed from them by just telling them their time is up!
"I will ascend above the heights of the clouds; I will be like the Most High." (They dress like the righteous and claim to be worshippers of God and one of His prophets – Jesus.)

It is the Most High Allah (God) in Person Who is High above the clouds on a man-made planet from the earth. Its machination cannot be equaled by the devil scientists.

TOOK 20 YEARS

It took the original machinists twenty years to build the "Mother Plane" that you see today flying through space and stars at night at a speed and height that the devils cannot ever be able to attain. Isaiah, Chapter 14:13, 14 is the root of the prophecy.

In Thessalonians, Chapter 2:4-12, the description fits the white race well in their works of trying to ascend to outer space planets, and their religion, Christianity, and their calling the heads of the church, "Father."

So, my people, I warn you; do not be deceived by the devils and their great showing of tricks of which you may think them to be the equal of Allah (God) and the angels of Allah (God).

NOTE: The 2nd Chapter of Thessalonians says: that the coming of God is after the workings of Satan (the devils) "and with all their deceivableness of unrighteousness in them that perish; because they received not the love of the truth, that they might be saved." (Thessalonians 2:10)

It is the so-called Negroes who are referred to in the words: "they received not the love of the truth." (Whom the white race has deceived.) The truth that the so-called Negroes are afraid to believe is the Truth of the white race being the real devils, the ever enemies of Allah, the Prophets and the original nation of the earth. (The Black, Brown, Yellow and Red races.)

HURRY and JOIN onto YOUR OWN KIND. THE TIME OF THIS WORLD IS AT HAND!

AMERICA'S DOOM

They say that they (White race) love the scriptures of the prophets of God and are followers of Jesus; then let that which they claim to believe be their judge. If they claim to be believers (of which they are not) in the scriptures of Allah's (God's) Prophets (surely, they brought the truth and that which they predicted would come to the wicked and the righteous in the last days) the truth of them is made manifest in our time.

America's price that she must pay for her evils done to her slaves (the Lost-Found members of the original nation of Islam from the Tribe of Shabazz) who are nicknamed "N e g r o e s" by the slave masters, is the same as that price paid by Pharaoh and his people.

MUST REAP WHAT IS SOWN

The only difference is that Egypt still exists, while America will not. She must reap what she has sown. She hates her Black slaves. She takes pleasure, daily, in robbing, beating and killing them, as though her Black slaves once robbed and killed them. Her hatred for her slaves can easily be seen and heard in the evil, filthy name-calling of the slaves.

She has never attempted to mistreat her aggressive nations, and those who war against her in such evil manners as she does her helpless slaves (so-called Negroes), who know nothing; only what their slave masers have taught them.

They are trying their best to imitate their teachers, the slave master. This is due to the born fear and ignorance of self and their masters.

They will fight to death for the independence of the slave master, but are too afraid to accept independence for self, or even to leave their slave master for a home among their own kind.

NOT LEARNED LOVE OF SELF

They have not learned love of self and kind as other nations;

they love their open enemy, the slave master, (the real devil). I still say that the history of Pharaoh could not have been made a better picture and warning to America and her slaves.

The very plagues, almost 100 percent, are mentioned and prophesied in the Revelations of John, the last book of the Bible, which brought an end to the symbolic "beast," except the fire does not run side by side with the water and hail, as in the case of Egypt under Pharaoh, according to both books, (Bible and Holy Qur'an).

Allah (God) used Pharaoh as a sign of the chief enemy's (devil's) destruction in the last Judgment of the opponents of God and the righteous.

Read the Bible Exodus 9:16-17 and see what Jehovah said to Pharaoh "and indeed for this cause have I raised thee up, for to show in thee my power; and that my Name may be declared throughout all the earth."

JEHOVAH'S WONDERFUL STORY

No reader of the Torah and Qur'an can say they overlooked this wonderful story of Jehovah's power, which crushed the power of Pharaoh in such manner as could be called a mockery of the proud king and his boast of power over Egypt and Israel, his slaves. It is the power of the White world that the world boasts they have that is powerful enough to destroy whoever tries to attack and destroy them.

America, since she hypocritically professes to be a believer in God and the Prophets will not say as Pharaoh said to Moses, for fear of losing the so-called Negroes who believe in the spooky slavery teachings of Christianity.

Today, America has the help of the Father (Pope) of the church, through the present administration in Washington, as we have never seen before. The Catholics are going all out, in America, to convert the so-called Negroes and the Black people in Africa.

Mocked the Idea

As Moses stood before Pharaoh representing Allah as the Lord of the Worlds, the proud wicked Pharaoh mocked the idea by suggesting that he would build a tower to attack Moses, God and Pharaoh said: O Haman, build for me a tower that I may attain the means of access to the heavens, that I may reach the God of Moses for I surely think him to be a liar." (Holy Qur'an 40:36, 37)

This "Haman" must have been Pharaoh's chief construction engineer of the war department. Note, that Moses made no mention that Jehovah never told Moses where He came from.

SIGN OF THE JUDGMENT

We must remember, that the judgment of this Pharaoh's rule and his people is a sign of the Judgment of the powerful rulers of today by the unequalled weapons that Allah has prepared to use in destroying them.

These terrible and dreadful weapons are, both, on the earth and in the heavens above the earth. Yet, these rulers mock the idea of Allah being able to destroy them and their advanced wicked science, without hurting one Muslim (the righteous).

The present wicked rulers have learned and now see, through their powerful telescopes, the power of Allah hanging and moving in the sky as well as you and I, who are able to see some of it with the naked eye.

Allah has made the retired ex-general, Keyhoe, take pictures of this power of Allah over our heads, which is almost identical to what Allah showed me in the sky in 1932.

Jesus prophesied of it coming in the clouds of heaven and Ezekiel gives us a faint picture of it in his vision of "a wheel in a wheel" high above the earth.

The foolish disbeliever of today, say and do the same as the disbelievers before them. Remember, Jehovah killed the mocking, proud Pharaoh, and his people for the evil they had done to Israel.

The symbolic prophetic "beast" of the Revelation was destroyed for his persecution of the symbolic "woman" and seeking to destroy her child at birth, Pharaoh and his people sought to destroy Israel by killing off all the boy babies; Herod sought to destroy Jesus by the same method.

What means, and methods are now in the working to destroy the so-called Negroes from becoming a ruling power. Watch for the answers! Remember, Israel was persecuted severely by Pharaoh and his people.

Rome and the Jews persecuted Jesus and his disciples. The Revelation's symbolic "beast" persecuted the symbolic "woman" and her child. The "Beast" and those with him were destroyed in a lake of fire. Pharaoh and his people were destroyed by drowning in the Red Sea. The Jews and Romans lost their independence and the power to rule the world.

What and how will America lose her power and independence to rule the world? Watch for the answer?

Hurry and join onto your own kind. The time of this world is at hand.

AN EVIL AND INDECENT RACE (WHITES)

The people of 'paradise' who followed Yakub 6,000 years ago had no idea that he intended to disgrace and destroy them. He was cast out and doomed to total destruction. He carried with him 59,999 original black people. This is the devil's same intentions today, to deceive and tempt the original black people here in America to go with them to THEIR CERTAIN DOOM. This is in the minds of white Americans' religious tempting and deceiving the so-called Negroes to make them deserving of hell fire with them. My people, I am warning you!

The Devils are now using one of their greatest weapons (temptation) to destroy the black people or cause them to take part in their doom which was prepared for them the very day they were created. They are aware of you, they see you, but you do not see them.

THOUGH ALLAH in these last few years has manifested them to you and me, your love for our enemies, the devils, is so great that you are blinded and cannot see them as devils. They are the enemies of God and the entire Black Nation.

REAL DEVILS ARE ENEMIES.

YOU DISPUTE the truth of them being the real devils – the enemies. You are even fools enough to teach the love and worship of them to your own children. It is a shame and a disgrace! You become so displeased with God and His servant for teaching you the truth of them that you call the truth "hate" or rather charge the Messenger of God with teaching you to hate white people! (the devils)

Your hopes in making such charge against the Messenger is that maybe the devils will put a stop to such true teachings – even by imprisoning or killing him and his followers as the enemies of God's Messengers did in the past.

I AM AFRAID you are going to be disappointed in your ignorant and wicked wish for your flesh and blood. Today, the bearer of truth is protected by his Sender, Allah to whom be praised forever. I only desire to see you saved from that which you have no part; only that which you take of yourself. I warn you against letting this evil tempter tempt you into their world of evil and indecency that you may share their doom.

FILTHY, WICKED SHOW

The so-called Christian race (the devils) is putting on one of their most filthy, most wicked shows that has even been produced by a human being. They sing filthy-love songs, filthy kissing and dancing, showing off their nude bodies and the television to your families to incite the evil, filthy, immoral practices into your children and yourself. The Bible and Holy Quran both warns us against accepting these devil's filthy temptations. Read Bible, Luke 8:13; James 1:12 Matthew 26:41; Deuteronomy 4:30; Revelation 3:10.

There is much more you may study that you might know the devils whom you in the past have not known; but now, the truth has come to us from the Lord of the Worlds! Why should they now tempt us after seeing and having knowledge of the evil, filthy-doings? The Christians or devils display NO shame.

THEY ARE bold and shyless, they are pig eaters, alcohol drinkers which help make them shameless, they go indecently dressed, according to the Holy Qur'an (7:17, 20, 21, 26.) And it (Qur'an) warns us of the shame devils deceived our fathers in "Paradise" 6,000 years ago. They (devils) led them out on an island in the Aegean Sea, stripped them of both the clothing that covered their shame and the wisdom and knowledge of themselves and God. And today they (the devils) are playing the same trick on you and me and the whole of the Black Nation.

READ THE FOLLOWING verses of the Holy Qur'an: "O Children of Adam, we have indeed sent down to you clothing to cover your shame and clothing for beauty, and clothing that guards against evil – that is the best." This is of the Messages of Allah that they may be mindful.

Let not the devils (the white race) seduce you, as he expelled your parents from the Garden, pulling off from them their clothing that he might show them their shame. He sees you, he as well as his host, from where you see them not, (electronic devices make this possible) surely we have made the devils to be the friends of the disbelievers." – (7:26, 27).

BATTLE IN THE SKY IS NEAR

The vision of Ezekiel's wheel in a wheel is true if carefully understood. There is a similar wheel in the sky today which very well answers the description of Ezekiel's vision. This wheel corresponds in a way with the spheres of spheres called the universe. The Maker of the universe is Allah (God) the Father of the Black Nation which includes the Brown, Yellow, and Red people. The Great Wheel which many of us see in the sky today is not so much a wheel as one may think in such terms, but rather a plane made like a wheel.

This wheel-like plane, it's like was never before seen. You cannot build one like it and get the same results. If you would make one to look like it, you could not get it up off the earth into outer space. The similar Ezekiel's wheel is a masterpiece of mechanics. Maybe I should not say the wheel is similar to Ezekiel's vision of a wheel, but that Ezekiel's vision has become a reality. His vision of the wheel included hints on the Great Wisdom of Almighty God, Allah; that really, He is the Maker of the universe, and reveals just where and how the decisive battle would take place (in the sky).

When guns and shells took the place of the sword, man's best defense against such weapons was a trench (ditch). Poison gas and liquid fire brought him out. Today, he has left the surface for the sky to destroy his enemy by dropping and exploding bombs on each other. All this was known in the days of Ezekiel, and God revealed it to him, that through Ezekiel, we might know what to expect at the end of this world.

The Originator and His people, the Original Black People are supremely wise. Today, we see the White Race preparing for the sky battle to determine who shall remain and rule this earth, Black or White. In the battle between God and the disbelievers in the days of Noah, the victor's weapon was water. He used fire in the case of Sodom and Gomorrah. In the battle against Pharaoh, He used ten different weapons which included fire and water, hailstone and great armies of the insect world and droughts and finally plagued them with death.

The Holy Qur'an says that: "the chastisement of Pharaoh was like that which God would use against His enemies in the last days."

Throughout the Bible—and Holy Qur'an teachings on the Judgement and destruction of the enemies, fire will be used as the last weapon. The earth's greatest arms are fire and water. The whole of its atmosphere is made up of fire and water and gases. It serves as a protected coat of arms against any falling fragments from her neighbors. Ezekiel saw wheels in the middle of a wheel. This is true: (the universe in the universe. It is made up of revolving spheres). There are wheels in the wheel.

The present wheel-shaped plane known as the Mother of Planes, is one half mile by one half mile and is the largest mechanical man-made object in the sky. It is a small human planet made for the purpose to destroy the present world of the enemies of Allah. The cost to build such a plane is staggering! The finest brains were used to build it. She is capable of staying in outer space six to twelve months at a time without coming into the earth's gravity. It carries fifteen hundred bombing planes with the most deadliest explosives: the type used in bringing up mountains on the earth, the very same method is to be used in the destruction of this world.

The bombs are equipped with motors and the toughest of steel was used in making them. This steel drills and takes the bombs into the earth at a depth of one mile and is timed not to explode until it reaches one mile into the earth. This explosion produces a mountain one mile high; not one bomb will fall on water. They will all fall on cities. As Ezekiel saw and heard in his vision of it (Chapter 10:2) the plane is terrible. It is seen but do not think of trying to attack it. That would be suicide!

The small, circular made planes called flying saucers, which are so much talked of being seen, could be from this Mother

Plane, of which Mr. Keyhoe claims in his book that he saw. This is only some of the things in store for the White man's evil world. Watch and read this article for it is the truth. Believe it or believe it not. This is to warn you and me to fly to our Own God and people.

Hurry and join onto your own kind

CORRUPTION

"Corruption has appeared in the land and sea on account of that which men's hands have wrought, that Allah may make them taste a part of that which they have done, so that they may return." – (Holy Qur'an 30:41)

THE WORLD approaches one of its most darkest periods since the creation of the Caucasian race; the intensity of it is increasing hourly. A high temperature of madness is troubling the heads of the nations, regardless to the great advancement of science in every field of wisdom. The great progress that they have made should bring joy and happiness, but instead of joy and happiness, trouble, sorrow, fear and trembling—and the worst is yet to come!

There is a great financial waste on a mad war race, arms that are made today, become obsolete tomorrow. Every nation is trying for the best and for the most destructive weapons of war. Billions of dollars are being spent on useless experiments; the currency is all but worthless. The great army of informers, nearly everyone will deceive the other. The above verse says that it is "On the account of that which men's hands have wrought." Man makes his own happiness or trouble. With his brain, he is able to think the thought or idea. He then forms an image of it and the ears, eyes, and mouth bear witness; then the hands fashion into shape, the image of the mind.

SO, THE WHITE RACE has prepared their own DOOM with their own hands, the great fortification at sea, and land. The prevailing corruption on the islands of the seas. The great mistake made by the White man, was in bringing the so-called Negroes from their native land and people, putting them in chains, to rob them of the knowledge of self and labor; and administering merciless beatings and killings for four hundred years. Now, the God of Justice says; as Thou has done, so shall it be done unto you.

ALLAH (GOD) has chosen the so-called Negroes to be His people and offers them heaven at once on their submission to His Will. He invites them into the true religion of God; "Then set thyself, being upright, to the right religion before there comes from Allah, the day which cannot be averted; on that day, they will be separated." (Holy Qur'an 30:43)

The Day mentioned, that cannot be averted is the day of DOOM for the enemies of Allah. There is no future for the so-called Negroes in the White man's world. For four hundred years, the slave-master and their children have not offered them anything but a job, work and serve them. Twenty million people cannot depend on a job in the factories and on the farms of White people, which benefits the owners, not the so-called Negroes. We must have some of this Earth that we can call our OWN. There we can create our own jobs, and the labor will benefit the Negroes. The slave-masters and their children have never given the slaves (the so-called Negroes) a fair chance to go for self.

They have not had an equal opportunity, and probably will never get one, as long as the White man is in power. The White man is against equal justice and equal opportunity for the Black man.

LAST WEEK, a Mr. George E. Sokolsky, news writer, seemed to be angry and upset over the progress that the Truth (Islam) is making among the so-called Negroes. Mr. W. D. Fard, Whose proper name is Allah, has brought this truth to awaken the so-called Negroes into the knowledge of self, God and the devil, and Mr. Sokolsky charges the progress of this truth to be from a violator of the narcotics law, who served three years in San Quentin Penitentiary.

NOTHING COULD BE WORST THAN THESE CHARGES! We will make Mr. George E. Sokolsky prove this lie, regardless to the cost! Allah (God) has brought the knowledge of the truth to us, and this truth is preventing our people from practicing their evil habits. The devil wants to stop the so-called Negroes from believing the truth.

HURRY and join onto your own kind. The time of this world is at hand.

DECEIVED

We now are seeking the respect of the Nations of the earth. To get this respect or recognition, we must lay aside many old, ignorant habits practiced from birth.

Keep the body and mind clean. Take frequent baths. A total bath should be taken daily. Stop eating swine flesh. It is a Divinely prohibited flesh. Two-thirds of our ailments can be traced to the eating of this poisonous animal called the swine (Hog). Go cleanly dressed. If you have only one suit, keep it clean. Keep your house clean. The woman should never invite or allow strange men to come into her home in the absence of her father, brother, (the son of her father) or husband.

Show respect to self and others. Respect and honor men in authority, whether they respect you or not. Provoke no one. Do not steal nor take advantage of one another because of the freedom to do so. Do not quarrel and fight each other, for we are brothers—same flesh and blood. Would you like to continue destroying your own flesh and blood? Protect your daughters and women from doing evil and filth. Protect them from the love of strange/men. Rid yourself of laziness—be smart and industrious regardless to whom or where. Be not wasteful, help to build a better future for self and kind.

Patronize your own people's business. Spend your dollars among your own kind. Serve One God, Allah, One religion— Islam. Be not divided, have love and unity of brotherhood first among yourselves. Help to secure a home on this earth that we can call our own. Do something for self and kind in the way of building a better future where we can enjoy peace and security, free from the shadow of death of our enemies.

I am so sorry that illness last Sunday, the 25th of June 1961 prevented me from keeping my appointment with you in the Nation's Capital. Allah is the Best Knower.

I have made visits and have mixed with our people (most all of them) and the above habits are the things being practiced by us that they (Nations) do not like, along with the love of our enemies and the hatred of self and kind.

HURRY AND JOIN ONTO YOUR OWN KIND. THE TIME OF THIS WORLD IS AT HAND.

DOOM OF AMERICA

America has been looked upon by the great scientists and scholars of the world as the greatest; the abundantly rich and prosperous nation. At the same time, they are the most wicked of all nations upon earth. America is a country that has been studied from both its industrial and scientific development and also from its moral and spiritual standards. America has been styled as a great factory: manufacturing products in great bulks and quantity to feed and satisfy its already wealthy who want to stay that was while the layman is a prey to America's ideas of monopoly and competition in the business of the political and social world. In reality, this is a "dog eat dog" country.

America is a gambling den and a refugee camp for criminals of all description: prostitutes, dope addicts and racketeers jam the cities from coast to coast from North to South. Wherever the White man goes, he invests large financial backings to contaminate and control the societies of countries such as South America, Africa, Asia and the Islands of the Seas, with the same evils and filth. He (White man) controls the engineering of America's power machines—the same enemy who has deprived the so-called Negroes the right to live as free people in this country. The so-called Negro cannot be classified on an equal basis with other minority people of foreign descent. You must remember that the Jews and other European and English immigrants (Italian, Spaniards, etc.) are first classified as being Caucasian, members of the White race; but the so-called Negro is a Black man and is identified as a piece of property, belonging to White America to do with as she pleases.

The so-called Negro had his beginning in this country as servitude slaves, who in the eyes of his master, was the same as his workhorse and cattle stock. Today, his status has moved up a little—from a servitude slave to a free slave. Now is the time for us to cut all chains of the master's grip and seek self-independence on this earth! Knowing that the White race continue daily to beat and lynch your brothers, rape and abuse your sisters, you yet cling to them. Who is it that has power over the beast to grab the beastly murderers, lynchers and assaulters by the neck and bring him to naught?

Who is it that can save the poor adult (who is yet a child to the knowledge of his enemies) from the White man's rope, gun, prison houses and other tools and weapons of destruction? No one but Almighty God, Allah, could put in me the undying spirit to try to awaken you to these truths before it is too late. We are fulfilling a period in history, known as the spiritual resurrection. No one but Almighty Allah could guide me to warn you of the great and dreadful day of the Lord which approaches near each fleeting moment. I have your key to the Judgment and to Paradise.

The so-called Negroes must stop taking lightly the daily abusive treatment of our people. You must work to prepare yourself and your family for a new day. You must stand up and tell the entire world of Asia, Africa, Europe and America that you are nobody's fool or tool any longer. You must begin to bear witness to the truth of Almighty God's religion—Islam, the true religion of the Black people, even though you are not able to live the righteous life of the Muslim nor stand by the unequaled principles of Islam.

The White man of America is well informed through his scientists and scholars, who are paid just for studying the problems of prophecy and especially the future destruction of America which he knows is fast coming. His greatest mental burden and physical strain at the present time, is how to prevent the spread of Islam among his "X" servitude slaves in these last days. The White man vividly recalls the story of the flood in Noah's day, the swallowing of Pharaoh's Army by the mighty Red Sea, the destruction of Sodom and Gomorrah, and the destruction of ancient Babylon, due to the conflict between the God of Good and the Devil.

The White man is well aware as to which category he fits. Now, they (White race) know that the hour draws near for their destruction and their entire civilization of wickedness. He knows that he represents the modern version of the people of Noah and the flood, the modern army of Pharaoh, the modern people of Sodom and Gomorrah and that modern "Mystery" Babylon referred to in Revelation.

HURRY AND JOIN ONTO YOUR OWN KIND. THE TIME OF THIS WORLD IS AT HAND!

FREE SLAVE? —FREE MASTER?

In unity, we can accomplish much. Think of the twenty million of your and my kind putting one dollar a year in a national treasury towards the day of want. Suppose we laid aside one dollar every month against the day of want. Look at the millions that we could build up for ourselves within a few years. Suppose all of you who are wealthy would spend your wealth to build up a better and more sound economic system among your own people. It would do much to aid our people. Do not put your wealth in the taverns, gambling houses, on race horses and other sports. Then, you would not be so easy to push over when the day of want arrives.

There is no need for us, millions and millions throughout the country, spending our money to the joy and happiness of others. As a result, as soon as they throw us out of a job, we are back at their doors begging for bread and soup. How many clothing shops do we operate in the country? Yet, all of us wear clothes. Who made our clothes for us? Who sold them to us? We have thousands of grocery stores. But what about our naked bodies? Should not we have stores to sell our people everything they want or need? But no! We give all the money out of our pockets over to the slave master. We are satisfied in doing so.

There are millions of us. We don't have a factory to weave clothes for our people here in America. Think over that. Where is our shoe factory? Where are our cattle that we are skinning the hides off to make shoes for our people? These are small things—but we want equality with a nation that is doing these things.

We boast that we should be recognized as equals with the master until we own what the master owns. We cannot be equal with the master until we have the freedom the master enjoys. We cannot be equal with the master until we have the education the master has. Then, we can say, "master, recognize me as your equal."

Today, you are begging the master, the slave master's

children for what? You are begging them for a job. You are begging for complete recognition as their equal. Let us be honest with ourselves. According to history, we cannot find where the master made his slave equal until the slave made himself worthy of equality.

I am with you to go on top. We cannot go on with weight that is hanging on us. We cannot charge the White man with our faults. We are supposed to be, according to his own teachings, free. We are supposed to have been freed from him approximately one hundred years ago. Have we exercised that freedom? We must answer that we have not availed ourselves of that freedom. If we have not availed ourselves of that freedom which he says he gave us, why should we think hard of him about the way he treats us? This may be a little hard to swallow.

Our fathers, in the days they were set free by the slave master, had no knowledge of how to go for self. They had been made blind, deaf and dumb to the knowledge of their own. Today, you are educated. You claim that you have equal education. Then, why don't you take a walk? Before we can be justified in accusing the other man, let us examine ourselves first. I don't say that our fathers are the ones to blame for their ignorance and neither are you. They nor you are at fault. The root of the cause can be placed back into the laps of the slave master. When the slave master says we are free and continues to say that we are free, should we not take a free step?

We charge the slave master's children with mistreating us. Suppose you tell a man that he is free. "Get out of our house and go into your own," but the freed slave says, "No, no. I'll work for you. I'll serve you as a servant if you will allow me to remain in your house." The man of the house tells you, "I won't give you a new suit this year. I'll not pay you today for any work. Go home and sit down." Why should you say that man is not treating you right? Why say to that man, "I have to have a job same as you?" Has not he offered the door to you?

If the slave master did not mean that you and I were free, we should have them to admit it. You remain as a free slave to your slave master. You demand that he recognize you as his equal.

You are making yourself look small in the eyes of the world. If every so-called Negro were fired, what would you do? Would you unite and go to Washington and demand the government to give you a job? You would be foolish enough to do that! If they beat you by the thousands, what right have you to say that he should not lash you? You have made yourself his slave. You continue to preach a doctrine of remaining with the slave master.

You are still called by your slave masters' names. By rights, by international rights, you belong to the White man of America. He knows that. You have never gotten out of the shackles of slavery. You are still in them. You are still in authority over your wife as long as she goes in your name, regardless of her separating herself from you. If she has not gotten a legal divorce and freed herself from your name, you are still in authority over her by law. Likewise, you are still under authority of the chains of your slave masters. You have not tried to free yourself from them. You have not exercised the freedom that they claim to have given you.

Today is "The Day of Decision." We have lived here more than four hundred years. That you know, according to prophecy, is the prediction of our stay among these people. That time has expired. The time is up. The decision is being made for your and my departure. It is most important to God Almighty, whose proper name is Allah, that I speak to you according to the time that we are living now.

Today, you are standing face to face with the alternative of accepting your own or forever be erased from the earth as a people. No one is trying to make you see this importance but your own. Why don't you see? You are blindly looking toward the slave master to tell you this. How can the master tell the slave, "Look, slave, your day has arrived. You should sit in this seat of authority." We cannot, cannot build a future on a job that was given to us by the slave master four hundred years ago. The day has arrived. He has no more work for us to do. He is not willing to tell us that. The time has arrived when deeply within his own heart, he desires that you go out and find a job for yourself. He will forever be burdened. The burden will get greater and greater as long as he tries to carry you and I. It is time for a separation of the two, Black and White. Allah. God is calling for a SEPARATION!

GET KNOWLEDGE TO BENEFIT SELF

I am for the acquiring of knowledge or the accumulating of knowledge, as we now call it in education. First, my people must be taught the knowledge of self. Then and only then will they be able to understand others and that which surrounds them. Anyone who does not have a knowledge of self is considered a victim of amnesia or either unconsciousness and they are not very competent. The lack of knowledge of self is a prevailing condition among my people here in America. Gaining the knowledge of self makes us unite and put us into a great unity. Knowledge of self makes you take on the great virtue of learning.

Many people have attempted to belittle or degrade my followers by referring to them as unlettered or unschooled. They do this to imply that the believers in Islam are ignorant. If such a claim were so, then all the more credit should be given for our striving for self-evaluation with so little. But truth represents itself and stands by itself. No followers, or any people are more zealous about the acquiring of knowledge than my followers. Throughout the Holy Qur'an, the duty of a Muslim to acquire knowledge is spelled out.

My people should get an education which will benefit their own people and not an education adding to the "storehouse" of their teacher. We need education but get an education which removes us from the shackles of slavery and servitude. Get an education, but not an education which leaves us in an inferior position and without a future. Get an education but not an education at the sacrifice of not learning the knowledge of self. Get an education but not an education that leaves us looking to the slave master for a job.

Education for my people should be where our children are off to themselves for the first fifteen or sixteen years in classes separated by the sex. Then they could and should seek higher education without losing respect for self or seeking to lose their identity. No people strives to lose themselves among other people except the so-called American Negro. This they do because of their lack of knowledge of self.

We should acquire an education where our people will become better students than their teachers. Get an education which will make our people put to better use the knowledge they acquire, that will make our people produce jobs for self and will make our people willing and able to go do for self. Is this not the goal and aim of many foreign students who are studying in this country? Don't these students return to their own nations and give their people the benefit of their learning?

Did not Dr. Nkrumah return to Ghana to lead his people to independence with the benefit of learning he acquired here in America and elsewhere? Did not Dr. Hastings Banda return to give the benefit of his education to his people, who are striving toward freedom and independence, **in Nyasaland? Did not Azikiwe Abubakar of Nigeria give the benefit of his education to the upliftment** and independence of his people? **Does not America offer exchange scholarships to** smaller, weaker and dependent foreign governments so their students will acquire knowledge to aid the people of those countries? Then why shouldn't the goal in education be the same for you and me?

Why is scorn and abuse directed towards my followers and myself when we say our people should get an education which will aid, benefit and uplift our people? Any other people would consider it a lasting insult, of the worst type, to ask them to refrain from helping their people to be independent by contributing the benefit of their knowledge.

Get an education, but one which will instill the idea and desire to get something of your own, a country of your own and jobs of your own.

I recall in 1922 or 23, when a debate was taking place in Congress concerning appropriation of funds for Howard University, a school set aside to train my people in the Nation's Capital, a senator said, it is in the records to be examined in effect, what would be the need of the government appropriating money to educate Negroes? He said they would not teach our people the science of modern warfare (defense), birth control or chemistry. He knew those were things free people must know in order to protect, preserve and advance themselves. We have not been able to protect, preserve and advance ourselves. This shows the slave master has been successful in dominating us with an education beneficial to him. There is a saying among us: "Mother may have, father may have, but God blesses the child who has its own." It is time we have our own!

I want an education for my people that will let them exercise the right of freedom. We are 100 years up from slavery. We are constantly told that we are free. Why can't we take advantage of that freedom? I want an education for my people that will elevate them. Why should we always be lying at the gate begging for bread, shelter, clothing and jobs if we are free and educated? Do not get an education just to set some useless symbolic monument to the Black man in the Western Hemisphere. We need an education that eliminates division among us. Acquire an education that creates unity and makes us desire to be with our own.

The acquiring of knowledge for our children and ourselves must not be limited to the "three R's" (reading, 'riting and 'rithmetic). It should instead, include the history of the Black nation, the knowledge of civilization of man and the universe and all the sciences. It will make us a greater people of tomorrow.

We must instill within our people the desire to learn and then use that learning for self. We must be obsessed with getting the type of education we may use towards the elevation and benefit of our people—when we have such people among us, we must make it possible for them to acquire this wealth which will be beneficial and useful to us.

One of the attributes of Allah, The All Wise God, Who is The Supreme Being, is knowledge. Knowledge is the result of learning and is a force or energy that makes its bearer, or a people accomplish or overcome obstacles, barriers and resistance. In fact, God means possessor of power and force. The education my people need is that knowledge, the attribute of God, which creates power to accomplish and make progress in the good things or the righteous things. We have tried other means and ways and we have failed. Why not try Islam? It is our only salvation. It is the religion of Allah, His prophets and our forefathers. Islam will let you take that step for self.

HURRY AND JOIN ONTO YOUR OWN. THE TIME OF THIS WORLD IS AT HAND.

"HAVE WE QUALIFIED MEN AND WOMEN FOR SELF-GOVERNMENT?"

The answer to this question is YES. We do not have to be equal in knowledge with every nation to be successful in operating our own government. Were those Israelites 4,000 years ago the Egyptian's equals? Were those whites who first came to this country seeking self-government equal to England's Parliamentary Lords?

There are probably many independent people who do not have as many with the "know-how" of the American educated class of so-called Negroes.

We have enough technicians such as mathematicians, construction engineers, civil engineers, mechanical engineers, physicists, chemists, educators, agriculturists, navigators, and aeronauts, among the 20 million or more of us.

PLENTY OF SCHOLARS, SCIENTISTS

You will find scholars or scientists we can use in every branch of government; then, there are our own independent people outside of this country who would be glad to help us get going in a country or state to ourselves. We do not expect or desire to build a government patterned after that of the white man.

Naturally, we would need help for the next 20 or 25 years; after that, we should be self-supporting! The spirit of "doing for self" is now fast coming into our people. They need a new education of self and others.

United under the crescent of Islam is all that is necessary for you and me to become the world's greatest people. The lying and slavery teachings of the white man's Christianity that has crucified our people over the earth must be given up! We must accept the true religion (Islam) of Jesus and the Prophets before and after him before we can be successful in doing anything.

WE HAVE NO FUTURE

Let the foolish educators and teachers think not that we have a future in white America's promises. For they themselves do not have a future, unless they are willing to divide this country between our people (so-called Negroes) and the Indians, whom they robbed nearly 500 years ago. However, we must have some earth that we can call our own and soon.

We, also the Indians, deserve justice in this matter! We can no longer think in the slavery-time terms that we used to think. The preachers need and must be taught the true religion of God and stop enslaving our people into that lying and slavery-teaching of the devils (white race).

Believe it or not, we have been serving and worshipping the REAL DEVILS! STOP preaching that old lie that God loves all human beings. He most certainly does NOT love the devils (the white race). He set a day for their doom the day they were grafted and given 6,000 years to rule us. A rule of lying and murdering us day and night and deceiving nearly the entire nation of Black, Brown, Yellow and Red people.

I possess a letter that is supposed to be authentic on how the devils boast of how they have murdered (killed) 100,000,000 black Africans since they have contacted them with their lying Christianity.

Do we not love our black brother's blood regardless to where spilled?

LIST OF MURDERS

In 1898, a devil by the name of Lacroix, representing Belgium's "big business," admitted he had murdered 160 so-called Negro men, women and children. He also admitted he had tortured some and crucified women and children.

THE CONGO: In 1880, Belgium estimated a population of 80,000,000. By 1911, the population was reduced to 20,000,000 by 1960 the population was 13,000,000.

In 1894 an English traveler, E.J. Glave reported: "Twenty-heads of black men were brought to Stanley Falls and used as decorations around a flower bed in one of the homes of a high-ranking army officer. Missionaries reported that white Christians forced the Negroes into slavery producing rubber.

And if the rubber was of bad quality, the poor black slaves were made to eat it. And you are fools enough to preach their deadly-poisoned religion, Christianity, to the suffering of self and kind. Are you in love with your open enemies, and murderers of all black people, God and His Prophets? Then stick around and see where you will end up!

"HAVE WE QUALIFIED MEN AND WOMEN FOR SELF-GOVERNMENT?" II

"And the devil will say when the matter is decided: Surely Allah promised you a promise of truth and I promised you then failed you. And I had no authority over you, except that I called you and you obeyed me. So, blame me not but blame yourselves. I cannot come to your help nor can you come to my help. I deny your associating with Allah before."-Holy Qur'an 14:22

The above verse is being fulfilled. The false leadership of the lost-found members of the Asiatic Nation from the Tribe of Shabazz, so-called Negroes, sincerely loves and worships the devils (white race) in such manner that should be due only to Allah (God).

The devils know that the so-called Negroes are fools for worshipping them as if they were equal to Allah. But the devils will not admit this until the truth forces them to admit that they are no equal to Allah. They will also admit that Allah's promise is true, but their promise is false even when they made it! But knowing that their followers (so-called Negroes) were blind, deaf and dumb to the knowledge and the truth of them, they could, therefore make false promises, and the blind, deaf and dumb would believe them.

WANT TO "SOCIALIZE"

So, it is today, the so-called Negro leadership is so desirous to socialize with the devils under the present act of "integration" that they forsake Allah (God) and His promise of truth – "of setting them in heaven at once!"

The so-called Negro seeks to hasten the devils to fulfill their promise of integration by telling the devils:

"If you don't hurry and fulfill that which you promised us,

the Muslims will take all of us." In other words, they are saying this:

"If you will do better by us than you have done in the past, then we will not accept Allah (God) and His Messenger, Elijah Muhammad. We love you and this world's life and will not follow anyone who does not love and follow you." But the devils will admit, after the truth is confirmed, that they have no authority over them, the so-called Negroes, (keeping them from believing in Allah, following His Messenger and the Teachings of Allah's religion, Islam) except that they (devils) called you (so-called Negroes) and you obeyed them.

AFRAID TO DISOBEY

The poor, fearful, disbelieving so-called Negroes are too afraid to disobey their known murderers (white Americans). But today, it is different. Obey the call of Allah and disobey the devils who have no power over you if you submit to Allah. The day is very near when you and the devils whom you take for friends will not be able to help each other against Allah.

In fact, and you see it today, any opposition to the teaching of Islam is not prosperous. It is the aim of Almighty Allah (God) to make His religion of TRUTH to triumph over all other religions, even though the believers of other religious may be against it (Islam). See Holy Qur'an 61:8,9.

WATCH YOUR "FRIENDS"

The Holy Qur'an Chapter 9:23, 24 warns the Muslims of taking even their disbeliever parents for friends in these words: "O you who believe, take not your fathers and your brothers for friends if they love disbelief above faith, and whoever of you takes them for friends, such are the wrong doers.

"If your fathers and your sons and your brethren and your wives and your kinsfolk and the wealth you have acquired and trade whose dullness you fear, and dwellings you love are dearer to you than Allah and His Messenger and striving in His way, then wait until Allah brings His command to pass."

There are many who would believe the truth (Islam), but their love for their disbelieving near of kin and friends are greater than their love for Allah and the truth. This lack of love for Almighty Allah (God) will cause them to go to hell with the disbelievers.

HURRY and JOIN YOUR OWN KIND. THE TIME OF THIS WORLD IS AT HAND!

HELP SELF BEFORE HELPING OTHERS

Many of my people, the so-called Negroes, say we should help the victims of Africa which are awakening. This has been said, as if we owned America. We are so foolish! What part of America do you have that you can offer towards helping Africa? Who is independent, the nations of Africa or we? The best act would be to request the independent governments of Africa and Asia to help us. We are the ones who need help. We have little or nothing to offer as help to others. We should begin to help at home first.

We are twenty million strong. Many of the nations today that have their independence are smaller in number than my people here in America. Just South of America is Cuba, which has a little over six and one-half million people. They are independent. We are more than three times their number and are not yet exercising the steps of freedom. We are dependent on the slave master. We do not have two feet of earth for our people. They also have independence. Remember, that we are numbering over twenty million and we have nothing!

Peru has close to ten million people and they have independence. Sudan has a little over ten million; Liberia has about ten million, the Congo has about twelve million; Tunisia has about four million and Afghanistan has about twelve million people and all are independent. Even in this hemisphere, the West Indies, with close to three and one-half million people, have gained their independence.

You and I, here in America, are licking the boots of the slave master, begging him for rights of independent people. Yes! We are licking his boots. 'Sir let me shine your shoes?' You have been doing that for approximately four hundred years. Today, if one rises up in your midst and says, "We should not lick the slave masters', we should lick our own boots," you say, "He should be killed because he is teaching us to hate." My people, you are in a dangerous position. Get out of your fear and stand up for your people! Who are you not to die for your people? Who am I not to die for my people? If I am shot down or cut down today, who is little Elijah Muhammad to twenty million of you? If a million of us throw ourselves in the fire for the benefit of the twenty million, the loss would be small compared to the great gain our people would make as a result of that sacrifice. Hundreds of thousands of Muslims gave their lives in Pakistan to get their freedom and independence. They were successful. The black man in Africa is fighting and dying today, in unity for their independence.

We sit here like pampered babies. We cannot even stand up on the floor; not to think about taking a chance of crawling out of the door. We are too careful of shedding blood for ourselves. We are willing to shed all of it for the benefit of others. I am not trying to get you to fight. That is not even necessary, our unity will win the battle. Not one of us will have to raise a sword. Not one gun would we need to fire. The great canon that will be fired is our unity. Our unity is more powerful than any atomic weapon or hydrogen bomb. All we have to do is unite. Our unity is the best. Why are you afraid to unite? Why are you afraid to accept Allah and Islam? It is only because the slave master did not teach you of this! We must unite as a nation of people!

Separation of the so-called Negroes from their slave masters' children is a must. It is the only solution to our problems. It is the only solution, according to the Bible, for Israel and the Egyptians. Separation will prove to be the only solution for America and her slaves, whom she mockingly calls her citizens, without granting citizenship. We must bear in mind, at all times, that we are being mocked.

You must know that this is the time of our separation and the judgement of this world (the Caucasian), which you and I have known. Therefore, Allah (God), has said to me that the time is ripe for you and me to accept our own, the whole planet earth. Are you waiting for the Divine Destruction? Come! Let us reason together. First, in order for us to reason, you must have a thorough knowledge of self. Who is going to teach you the knowledge of self? Surely, not your slave master who blinded you to that knowledge. The slave master will not teach you the knowledge of self, as there would not be a slave-master relationship any longer.

Today, for the first time in our history, we have that True Friend in Allah (Who came in the person of Master Fard Muhammad) and the Nation of Islam. We have only to submit and accept Him. Allah (God) to Whom praise is due, is here to give you and me a superior knowledge of things and a country of ourselves.

HURRY AND JOIN ONTO YOUR OWN. THE TIME OF THIS WORLD IS AT HAND.

HELP SELF BEFORE HELPING OTHERS II

Do you have a name of Allah (God)? There are 99 names of Allah, and "Allah" makes the 100th. You owe it to yourself and your future to be called by one of Allah's names. So-called Negroes, who are the lost-found members of the Tribe of Shabazz, belong in one of the 100 names of Allah; and they owe it to themselves to hurry and get in His Name. The Bible makes this abundantly clear that those who are without the Name of Allah (God) will be the losers on the Day of Judgment (Isaiah 65:15; Revelation 14: 9, 10).

There are many who think a name means nothing. Those who believe a name means nothing are in great need of teaching. The first thing that is asked in getting acquainted with people is: "What is your name?" We are absolutely judged according to the value of our names. We have been the property of strange and wicked masters and they have called us by their names, which are not Divine Names. Their names are worthless and are not even human names; for example: fish, bird, wood, tree, Roundtree, sawyer, rivers, waters, and many others. There will be no one in his Hereafter who does not have a Name of Allah. As Allah's (God's) name is eternal, so must we, who are lucky to see the hereafter, have a name that will live forever.

The present names of the Muslims are names of Allah, some use His name "Allah." The names of this wicked race of devils are to be destroyed with them. (Isaiah 65:15; Revelation 14:11). There are many prophecies in the Bible on the total destruction of this wicked world as you and I know it to be. So be not too proud to seek a good name that will live forever – a Name of Allah's. Never forget that the Nation of Islam is infinite, the religion of Islam is the only religion accepted by God. Islam means entire submission to the will of Allah. Therefore, those who submit to Allah are called by His name and will live forever with Allah.

You don't see me or my followers going to the devil's courts to get permits to be called by one of the Names of Allah (attributes). This is by no means necessary! There is no price on a good name from Allah. Allah (God) wants to give you one of His eternal names if you will accept and submit to Him.

These present names you are being called in are not your names at all! They are the white devil's names. They call you after their names as their fathers did when you were their personal property (slave); but remember, you are not their personal property today! The coming of Allah has redeemed us; by nature, you are not a member of the devil race. But they wish to keep you in their worthless names because they know their race and names are limited on the earth, and your nation and Allah's names are unlimited. We are the real owners of the heavens and earth. It was our fathers who created it, not a white man.

You will soon come to know that we should be ashamed, after having the knowledge to be called after the names of our white slave masters; our open enemies of Allah and the righteous black people, whose future was limited to rule for 6,000 years. This time ended in 1914. The white race cannot help from doing evil, killing and doing injustices to each other – let alone you and me!

Be happy that the day is here that their evil doings shall be put to an end. The few ignorant (having not knowledge) Muslims who think that they (white race) are the people of Allah shall soon be made ashamed. The entire white race are the real devils by nature. If you are wise or would like to be made wise, get out of their names into one that shall live forever.

THE HOPEFUL AND THE HOPELESS

We must have faith in the truth when it comes to us. We, the so-called Negroes today, are divided into two classes; the hopeful and the hopeless. The two classes confuse each other. The poor uneducated under privileged, the victims of the lawless brute force of our enemies are the hopeful and they gladly hear the truth as it is written in Mark 12:37.

The intellectuals, the rich, the religious leaders and teachers of the old order are always the "die hards" with the rulers of the people (the so-called Negroes)- the Lost-Found members of the Tribe of Shabazz. Allah (God) is now opening their hearts for the acceptance of the truth: the knowledge of self and others, the true religion - Islam; the religion in which the Believers are rightly guided, backed and protected by the Author, Allah (God). The Truth (Islam) inspires hope in them for a better future in a better world where freedom justice and equality is the nature and rule of the people; where hypocrites and the murderers will not be tolerated. A future where every believer is the brother of the Believers and this is carried into practice every minute of the hour.

The poor wants freedom indeed. He wants equal justice, equal opportunity, and an equal chance to bring into practice every good faculty that is latent in him. He wants to live under a government of righteousness and where unjust judges and rulers will not exist; where the poor enjoys peace and security equally with the rich and the rulers of the land.

Allah, through their belief in Islam makes the once slaves to lift up their heads in pride, honor and respect. The once slaves are made to feel equal with their masters and is fired with the spirit of doing for self. He will want to be a servant for no one except Allah, to whom his life becomes dedicated. He now, for the first time, feels like a man with a true sense of self pride. He now has hope and is hopeful of his future. Now, as all other independent people, he wants some of this earth he can call his own, wherein he (and his people) can set up a government of his choice. This is the effect Islam has upon the Believers.

The hopeless are the rich and wealthy; teachers, educators, religious leaders and politicians; lovers and friends of the enemies of the poor. They have no hope in self, nor in their nation. Their hopes are in the robbers of their people (the white slave masters). They are qualified to start self-government except for having the knowledge of self. Many of them are experts in every avenue of the political sciences in government, whether they were given the chance to study and learn from the slave masters. But they just feel and believe that to try leaving their old slave masters and teachers will cause them to go to the bread line. They are hopeless. They would rather lick the boots of their masters than to leave their masters and demand some of this earth they can call their own wherein they can set up their own government to their own likeness.

We (20,000,000 so-called Negroes) cannot forever depend on the white race to make jobs for us and our children. We must prepare and qualify men of our own race to help lead and put our people in the paradise of self-rulership.

We have in you and in us-if united- the know-how to create and make jobs for ourselves and people! Why do we not do it? It is because of the enemy of hopelessness in the ability of self to do something for self! For too long we have been dependent upon the slave masters. Let us stand up as men and demand OR TAKE some of this earth for our 20,000,000 homeless whether the world like it or not! We must have a home on some of this earth we can call our own AND AT ANY PRICE.

KNOW THYSELF

There is now an effort to celebrate a so-called "Negro History Week" beginning February 12 and some of my people will participate. The planning of that week, to teach the slave a knowledge of his past is not complete, sufficient nor comprehensive enough to enable my people to learn the true knowledge of themselves. It is important that my people learn the true knowledge of self as it means their salvation.

We are not Negroes because God, Whose proper name is Allah, has taught me who we are. We are not "Colored" people because God has taught me who we are, and He has taught me who the "Colored" people are. The poor so-called American Negro is without a knowledge of self. You are a so-called Negro because you are not a Negro. Allah (God) has given to me our proper names, the people from which we were taken and brought here to the shores of North America and the history of our forefathers. Allah has taught me and today I do not fear to tell you, that you can discard that name "Negro." We are not "Negroes! We are not Colored"! Those are some of the main things which we should remember.

We must become aware of the knowledge of self and the time in which we are living. You must know these things whether you agree that Elijah Muhammad is on time or out of time. If what I say is out of season, it goes for nothing. If I am on time or in season, then all I say will bear fruit.

There is much misunderstanding among us because of our inferior knowledge of self. We have been to schools where they do not teach us the knowledge of self. We have been to the schools of our slave master's children. We have been to their schools and gone as far as they allowed us to go. That was not far enough for us to learn a knowledge of self. The lack of knowledge of self is one of our main handicaps. It blocks us throughout the world. If you were the world, and you are a part of the world, you would also turn a man down if he didn't know who he actually was. If we, the so-called Negroes, don't know our own selves, how can we be accepted by a people who have a knowledge of self?

If we are representing ourselves as Negroes and "Colored" people, how did we get these names? Where do we find the age or the record of Negroes and "Colored" people in the ancient history of the Black man? Your search of the ancient history of the Black man of the Earth will prove that not once in time were Negroes or "Colored" people living in Asia or Africa. How did we come by those names? The names are from the slave masters.

They have called us by their names and the nicknames used among themselves. It even seems that we like being called by the slave master's names. After nearly a hundred years of freedom, we are still representing ourselves by the names our slave master called us! We must learn that the slave master's names are not accepted by God nor by the righteous people of God.

It is time for us to learn who we really are, and it is time for us to understand ourselves. That true knowledge is here for you today whether you accept it or reject it. God has said that we are members of the original people or Black nation of the Earth. Original means **first**. Historian J.A. Rogers points out in his books that beyond the cotton fields of the South and long before the White man himself was a part of our planet, we were the original people ruling the Earth and according to The Holy Qur'an, we have governments superior than any we are experiencing today.

Trace over the Earth. Check back five, ten or twenty thousand years ago. Look at history. Who were those people? They were our people! Today, we are confronted with proof of who the original people are and who shall live on this Earth and call it their own.

HURRY AND JOIN ONTO YOUR OWN KIND. THE TIME OF THIS WORLD IS AT HAND.

KNOW THYSELF II

The first shall be the last! If we are the first people, and that is an undeniable fact, we shall be the last! We cannot find a people who were before the Black man. Beyond a shadow of doubt, the Black man was the first man in the sun. If we preach a doctrine today that the Black man will be the last and that he will come into power today, why should you be surprised? Should you be surprised to learn that the so-called American Negro is a member of that nation which was here trillions of years before the White race? Should you be surprised that we preach the Black man will be here after others are gone?

The original tree is stronger than its branches. We have been robbed, spoiled and buried under the rubbish heap. Allah has told me that we are the original people—we are the father of all races. If truth is called teaching supremacy, then it will have to stand! An examination will prove to the contrary. You will find White supremacy is taught to us in the North, South, East and West of America. It is a shame! The White race's achievements, history, inventions, discoveries, ownership, progressiveness and Godliness are from us, the original nation.

Some scholars say that we have come to the crossroads. They say that we have met on the "field of decision." I don't condemn them. I say, the so-called Negro has arrived at the day in which we must make our minds up to take our place alongside our own kind. We are in a day that we have no time for sport and play. Nor are we in a day that we should sit down, sing love songs or play games of chance. We are in a serious time! A time when the old world is going out and a new world is coming in.

The solution to our problem is separation from the White world. Some of us think that we cannot solve our problems unless we have it dictated by our slave-master's children. Those are the thoughts of you who have lost your heads. It is time that you know self and know that Allah (God) is in our midst, manifesting the time. You will soon come to know that there is no God, but Allah and I am His servant. Be yourself—Allah has said that you are the best, the powerful.

HURRY AND JOIN ONTO YOUR OWN KIND. THE TIME OF THIS WORLD IS AT HAND.

NO JUSTICE FOR SO-CALLED NEGROES

We await the day of April 18th when Judge W.M. Harper sentences eight Muslims whom Monroe police beat and brutally assaulted for worshipping in the religion of Islam. The police placed false charges against the Muslims to cover up their own disregard of the laws. It is stated in the U.S. Constitution that a person may practice any religion of his choosing, has the right of free speech and peaceful assembly without sanction by government authorities!

Police Chief James Kelly stated to several of the Muslims during investigation of the religion of Islam that he would not tolerate the religion of Islam in Monroe. The Muslims face one-year compulsory jail sentences and $500 fines each. Faced with the sentence, Islamic Teacher Troy X said, "There is no God but Allah and Muhammad is His Apostle."

The city officials of Monroe made an all-out effort to break the Muslim's spirit and means and ways for obtaining defense counsel. The Muslims were attacked in their Mosque, a religious place of worship in Islam, by the police armed with machine guns, tear gas and heavy caveman-like clubs. The unarmed Muslims were beaten, arrested and placed under false charges of assaulting police officers on Sunday, March 5th. Included among arrested were children and the four months pregnant Muslim wife of the Islamic teacher. The Muslims were unable to get attorneys in Monroe to defend them in court as the local authorities brought political pressure on the attorneys.

Every bonding company in Louisiana refused bonds to release the Muslims who were held in jail ten days. Muhammad's Mosque Headquarters in Chicago secured the services of Attorney James R. Venable of Atlanta, Georgia. The Headquarters Mosque place $1,500.00 cash as bail for the release of the Muslims. Attorney Venable was arrested after the trial for auto theft even though he is numbered among the wealthiest White men of Georgia. Veteran observers said these false charges against the attorney were further intimidations to prevent the Muslims' right to counsel. For four hundred years, we have been deprived of equal justice.

Mr. Patrick M. Malin, Executive Director, American Civil Liberties Union, wrote Attorney General Robert F. Kennedy to intervene. Mr. Malin stated, "If the facts as presented to us by the Muslim Group are correct, a violation of federal civil rights seems to have occurred."

Many legal experts doubted that the Justice Department would take serious note of the violations of the freedoms of religion provisions in the U.S. Constitution. Attorney General Kennedy had information on the Muslims before the trial and failed to guarantee their rights. All this is to prove that we have no justice under the American Flag.

HURRY AND JOIN ONTO YOUR KIND. THE TIME OF THIS WORLD IS AT HAND.

NO JUSTICE FOR US IN USA

We have wondered why white people hate and mistreat us after we have been so obedient, so submissive, with "hat in hand" and a scared smile or grin on our faces from ear to ear.

We have killed their enemies for them, and sometimes those whom they called their enemies were our own people. For 400 years, we've tried to understand why the white race here in America hate, beat and kill their helpless free slaves, and yet preach Jesus Christ and God's love and justice; but even those white preachers and priests, the Pope (Father of the church) have never untied and protested to the government against the lawless, upright beating and killing of us, the so-called American Negroes. (Members of the Tribe of Shabazz).

INJUSTICE INCREASED

Even today, while the government is offering integration, (which will not solve our problem, but make it harder to solve) injustice to us have increased!

And the so-called 'God-sent' white and black preachers of Christianity are not using their churches and followers to protest against these injustices. We are witnessing them go into a lake of fire. (the lake is none other than the entire continent of North against them, even the recent police brutality and murder of our people in Los Angeles, April 27, 1962.

We do not have united Christian preachers nor priests of the churches protesting against such unprovoked, lawless, outright murder of our people. Even, according to the Los Angeles Times and the Herald-Examiner newspapers, the black preachers spoke in sympathy with that ungodly, merciless, brute police force headed by the worst hater (William Parker) of the black people in this unjust government of America. Today, Allah is making them manifest to the world as a race of devils, made to be our enemies and murderers until the day of their doom (which is very near).

HITS FREE DEVIL MURDERS

Here in North America will the fire of hell take place first on those who sit and rejoice to see poor, innocent black men burned to ashes, as the hands of the free devil murderers of our people.

The black people of America must be given the knowledge of self and of these open, heartless devils whose aims today are to take the poor black people to hell with them, while at the same time give you as much death and hell at their hands before Allah takes them, into a lake of fire. (The lake is none other than the entire continent of North America).

They teach love, but this does not mean that they love you because of your belief in Christianity. NO! But rather that you love them – this will make you an enemy of God. I have warned you, the white race's name alone will get you hell from God. They would like that you believe as you have always, in that which they taught you – Christianity!

They call the Truth that I have received from Allah "hate teachings" because it makes them manifest. Who could love the devils after having the knowledge of them?

DELIVER POOR AND NEEDY

Read the following chapters and verses from your Bible, which refers to you and them: Psalms 82: 3, 4. "Do justice to the afflicted; deliver the poor and needy; rid them out of the hands of the wicked (the white devils of the U.S.A.). They (the black people of America) know not, neither will they understand, they walk on into darkness.

All the foundation of the earth is out of course. (Not the earth itself, but the governments of the wicked is out of a wise course.) Justice standeth afar off (for the so-called Negroes.) Truth is fallen in the streets (is not accepted).

"None calleth for justice (when it is for so-called Negroes, nor any pleadeth for the Truth; (They trust the devil's lies) the devils feet run to do evil, they make haste to shed innocent blood. (Kill a so-called Negro). Their thoughts are evil, wasting and destruction." (Isaiah 59:4, 9, 14.)

Let us unite and seek some of this good earth for a home that we can call our own! Leave a people who are daily bent upon your destruction, your disgrace and shame alone!

PEACE?

Can there be any peace for the peace breaker? Allah told me that six thousand years ago, this same people's father (white race) broke the peace of the righteous in the gardens of Eden (the place that is known as old Persia). They called the truth of God a lie and made lies the truth. They said to the people of the Garden, according to the Bible (Gen. 3:4-6), "And the serpent (a name used according to the evil, deceiving characteristics of the Caucasian race) said unto the woman, you shall not surely die; for God doth know that in the day you eat thereof, then your eyes shall be opened, and you shall be as gods..." The serpent lied, because they did die. And the deceiver (serpent) was driven out of the garden into the wilderness of the earth to build a wicked kingdom of evil to be destroyed on the coming of God.

They (the white race) are playing the same trick on the black nation today as they did in the days of Adam. They shall suffer eternal expulsion from this earth in a lake of fire (Revelation 20:10).

Can they enjoy peace? After they were cast of the garden, according to the Holy Qur'an 7:16, "Because thou have thrown me out of the way, Lo, I will lie in wait for them on the straight path in the days of the resurrection and judgment of this evil world. He swore to them in another place that he would lead them to a tree of immorality and a kingdom that decays not. This kind of teaching is found in the teachings of Christianity. It is a very clever way of deceiving the black people of America; for here, Satan represents himself as an angel of light. They paint a picture of lies of "beyond the grave," when they know there is no life or communication with the dead. All ceases to be life after death. This is universally known.

Can they have peace? When they were created to destroy the peace of the righteous, as it is written, "Destruction cometh; and they shall seek peace, and there shall be none, mischief shall come upon mischief and rumor shall be upon rumor;"

(Ezekiel 7:25). They wrongfully represent themselves as peacemakers and lovers of peace and freedom (but only for themselves). This kind of talk deceives the nations while at the same time they are the troublemakers. As it is written: "But the wicked are like the troubled sea when it cannot rest, whose waters cast up mire and dirt." So, it is with this wicked race whom God has permitted to become the richest and most progressed people of earth. The more they increase in riches and power, the more they seek to trouble those that are at peace with them. They envy the peace and progress of others and are never satisfied, though they have the world bowing at their feet. They are forever deceiving the poor so-called Negroes with false promises and the so-called Negroes seem to love it. There is no peace for the wicked saith the God of peace (Isaiah 57:20, 21). The only peace today is with Allah and in His only religion of peace, Islam. Believe it or leave it!

Hurry and join onto your own kind. The time of this world is at hand.

PEACE? II

Islam is the religion of entire submission to the Will of Allah (God). "Nay, whoever submits his whole self to Allah and is a doer of good – he will get his reward with this Lord; on such shall be no fear, nor shall they grieve." (Holy Qur'an 2:112)

That and that alone is Salvation according to the Holy Qur'an. Fear is the number one (1) enemy that is blocking progress and success from coming to the so-called Negroes of America. This fear causes them to grieve. The world knows the poor so-called Negroes of America have and still suffers more grief and sorrow than any people on earth. This fear is the fear of the slave masters (white men) and what the slave masters dislike.

Let the so-called Negroes submit to Allah (God), and they will not fear anymore, nor will they grieve anymore. As it is written: "The fear of man bringeth a snare." (Proverbs 29:25) The fear has surely snared the poor so-called Negroes.

The Lord of the world's, the Finder of we the lost members of the Asiatic Black Nation for four hundred (400) years said, the slave masters put fear in our Fathers when they were babies. Allah is the only one that can remove this fear from us, but He will not remove it from us until we submit to His will and not our will and fear Him, and Him alone. Then, as it is written: "And it shall come to pass in the day that the Lord shall give thee rest from sorrow, and from thy fear, and from the hard bondage wherein thou wast made to serve." (Bible: Isaiah 14:3). There are so many places that I could point out in the Bible and Holy Qur'an that warns us of fearing our enemies above or equal to the fear of Allah (God). It is a fool that has greater fear of the devils than Allah, who has the power to destroy the devils and their followers. (Bible: Revelation 21:8 – Holy Qur'an 7:18 and 15:43).

We must remember that if Islam means entire submission

to the will of Allah, that and that alone is the True religion of Allah. Do not you and your religious teachers, and the Prophets of old teach that the only way to receive God's help or Guidance is to submit to His will, then WHY NOT ISLAM! It (Islam) is the True religion and the only way to success.

HURRY AND JOIN ONTO YOUR OWN KIND. THE TIME OF THIS WORLD IS AT HAND!

ROBBED AND SPOILED

"They are all of them snared in holes, and they are hid in prison houses; they are for a prey, and none delivereth for a spoil, and none saith restore." (Isaiah 42:22)

If my people's condition, or rather history, in America is not the answer to the above saying of Isaiah, then try to find the answer to it elsewhere. Our fathers were brought here as merchandise to be sold on the slave market. Some, according to the white man's own written history of that account, were brought here in physical chains to be chained again mentally for four hundred years and they are still mentally chained. They are still beaten and killed without any law of Justice for them.

The white murderer's word is heard and believed by his brother murderer in the office and seat of Justice. The poor black man (his master's most loyal and faithful slave), his word is not heard. They are afraid of an arresting officer taking them under arrest for fear of being mercilessly beaten; skull and face bashed in or shot outright, and the white brother says: "What is it to kill a damn Negro?" They are outright murderers clothed with authority to mistreat and kill my poor Black People whom they have been murdering (all of their lives) for the past four hundred years. Even when their own people (Black) are put in authority and arrive on the scene with a gun and club, they will (in many cases) prove to be even worse and quicker to beat and kill their own people than the white officer. This they do to be befriended by the white people.

"Robbed and Spoiled": They are pitiful (robbed by all), no, not even spared by their priest (church preachers) (Luke 10:32). The same robbers rob them of their own women; disgrace and corrupt them with all kinds of diseases, besides spotting up her children like the animal family. They are robbed so completely that now, after four hundred years, they love the robbers of themselves, and their kind. After being completely robbed of the knowledge of their God, religion and people, they now are a prey in the hands of all first-rate robbers of all races and people.

Our open enemies, the devils, are now using every tricknology on my people, after hearing the Truth (Islam), in order to take them (Black People) to hell with them. There never was and never will be true friendship between White and Black people regardless to what you try doing to bring it about. Nothing will bring peace between the two but SEPARATION of them.

SEPARATION

WE MUST make jobs for ourselves. Newspapers and magazines are writing and telling of our people heading the unemployment lines, being fired off their jobs without the means of finding new gainful employment. No new jobs are being offered our people. Our people here in America number twenty million with more than seven million eligible for gainful employment.

Our number in America is the equal or exceeding many independent nations which sit in chambers of counsel. As a nation of people contained and suppressed in America, we must begin to think for ourselves and do the thing which is best for us. Many television news programs show our people in the relief lines and at the employment offices sitting and begging the slave master for his bread and jobs. We should be seeking something of our own. Our people will always be a nation of beggars until we get something of our own!

I stated at our mass public meeting last Sunday, at the International Amphitheatre, that the present administration of the government promised the so-called Negro employment. You do not have it. The so-called Negro put his faith in the promise of the present administration by pooling his votes for it. I stated at the meeting that if they had said they would give us a few states, Elijah would have voted for them. The best thing to do to solve the problem of the so-called Negro is to separate from the White race.

The work of Allah among the so-called Negro is to separate him from his slave-master and give him something of his own. Also, at the meeting in the International Amphitheatre, I called again for the separation of the so-called Negro instead of integrating him among the White race. We should be given two or three states, so we may have a land of our own. We should be given the proper instruments or tools to sustain and build up our own civilization. We should be given support to last our nation twenty years. After that time if we are not able to go for our self, the slave master should take his armies and kill us.

Many of the national television companies reported on their TV stations my call for the so-called Negro to be separated into a land of his own. One commentator said many so-called Negro leaders do not agree with me. Naturally, the so-called Negro leaders are afraid to ask for anything. The White man speaking for the Negro leader is another indication of their power and control over the ones who are supposed to be guiding and benefiting our people. We cannot depend on the White race for our future, with only a job in view.

We must be separated into a land of our own. Permanent employment lies in our having ownership of land. We can have lasting jobs on our own land, but not on the land of others. The jobs of the White man are the ones that he has created and built for his own people.

I am very happy and thankful to Allah (God) for more than 8,000 people who came to our public meeting last Sunday. I am especially thankful for my faithful following who travelled from all parts of North America for our Annual Savior's Day meeting for the commemoration of the birth of our Savior who came in the person of Master Fard Muhammad.

HURRY AND JOIN ONTO YOUR OWN KIND. THE TIME OF THIS WORLD IS AT HAND.

SEPARATION IS A MUST

The poor so-called Negroes (the lost-found people of the Black nation from the Tribe of Shabazz) in America, brought here by the White man in 1555; said Allah (God in person) the best knower that our fathers and mothers were brought in chains at a great loss of life. According to history, we have served them (our slave masters) well for the past four hundred years. According to the bible's history made by Abraham on receiving the prophecy of our enslavement in a strange land and people to serve for four hundred years.

America was not known to the White Europeans before Columbus discovery of the Western Hemisphere in 1492, four hundred and seventy years ago. Beyond a shadow of a doubt, this is the strange land, and the White race, a strange people to the original Indians and our father, who were brought here in 1555, four hundred and seven years ago, did not know either the people (White and Indian) nor the country. All were strangers.

If this is not the answer to Abraham's prophecy, then you may tell me. Today our unrest and longing for unity and love of self and kind, and the desire for freedom, justice, and equality, a home on this earth that we can call our own, and the presence of God among us, the giving and calling us after Divine names, is a true sign that we are the people that Abraham saw and prophesied that would be lost and must be found. The prophecy is mentioned in many places throughout the bible. It ends with the struggle between the symbolic lamb and beast over the delivering of the same people (the so-called Negroes in America) from a wicked, merciless murderer like a savage beast over a prey.

It is a must that we be separated from our Slaver Masters' children, who like their fathers, hate and despise us with murder and slavery in their hearts for us day and night. It is foolish and ignorant to hear any Black man or woman praising the offer of integration with a four-hundred-year-old enemy of ours, which is inviting death and destruction of both races. Not one offer to give the once slave land to build a government and nation of their own, where they can live without fear of being beaten and killed without justice. Our enemies go in gangs to kill you. They rejoice to do you harm, this you know.

They are not like you and me. Their father was a devil, who created them to be enemies of the Black people (the righteous) by the spirit of their father (which was false and murderous) so are they, and today they are deceiving you under false pretenses that they will do good by you just to share hell fire with them. My Allah will give us heaven if you will only believe and come follow me. We need a country to ourselves like all other nations, and we will get it soon.

"Separate, whereof ye can come out from among them and be ye separate, saith the Lord, and touch not the unclean (the wicked White race) and I will receive you and will be a father unto you and you shall be my sons and daughters, saith the Lord, Almighty." (2 Corinthians 6:17, 18) "And I heard another voice from heaven saying, Come out of her, my people that you be not partakers of her sins and that you receive not of her plagues." (Revelation 18:4)

HURRY AND JOIN UNTO your own kind. The Time of the world is at hand.

SEPARATION OR DEATH

Let us take a look at some of the disgrace that White America has committed against you, my people, and then let us look at the things they are doing now.

We know that during the Civil War, Negroes went into battle with their slave-masters—fighting to keep their South land enslaved. They felt as though they were justified. Their slave-master taught them that he (the slave-master) was fighting for what was right. He still thinks the same today.

Though uneducated, they (slaves) were like machines—controlled by the White man. Now, even though the South lost that war, they continue to control the Negroes. It was through the Negro Congressman, who were elected during the Reconstruction period following the Civil War, who helped pass many of the so-called "Jim Crow" laws. Today, the South still use these laws against our people. Don't get angry with them, for they thought that by passing those "Jim Crow" laws, they were protecting their people from the White man. But, time is a funny thing, for those laws reversed when the White man began to gain political office—by using fear and force on the potential Negro political officer seeker. He formed the three "K's" and with that, brought death to our people. You know that through fear, you can gain control over people and that control can be used to a person's advantage.

As the White man gained political control, he constantly passed state laws to make the Negro (even though they were freed by the Federal Government) feel as though they must still depend on the White man. He set up separate schools (but only taught his history). He set up his religious churches (Methodist and Baptist) but they too were still separated. They taught the Negro their religion (Christianity) so you could look to him for dependence. Now, he is still trying to make you dependent on him by saying, "I will give you Civil Rights," but he is still trying to make you dependent on him by saying, "I will give you Civil

Rights," but he thinks you don't realize that he promised you those rights when the 13th, 14th, and 15th Amendments, for Civil Rights, were passed in 1866.

Well, it has been approximately 100 years now and he still says, "We will give you rights, but don't be in such a hurry!" Brothers and sisters, how much longer do we have to wait—another hundred years? I say, White America doesn't want to give us complete freedom, justice and equality. They don't want to give us a piece of this country where we can have what so many of us died on the battlefields of this country (Civil War) and Europe for: a part of this country where our future kind can enjoy freedom, justice and equality and have an economy of our own; a country where we can worship in the true religion of our forefathers, which is Islam.

Islam is the only true religion of God (Allah). It is the religion of all His prophets, from Adam to Muhammad. Teach this (Islam) to your brothers and friends, your children and their children's children.

Build your future on freedom, justice and equality. Build it on a part of this good earth that we can all our own! Be "Freedom Riders" on your own soil! Seek to mix with your own Black kind keep your identity from being destroyed by the devils (White man). All they want to do is destroy your identity by offering you token integration.

Hurry and join onto your own kind. The time of this world is at hand!

SEPARATION OR DEATH II

What is it today that is pushing and forcing America to pass a law permitting the integration instead of the separation of Black and White? Does America see her doom? They understand the time of day while you do not. They know that it is the time of the judgment of Allah: to destroy the power of Satan's rule. The truth of their 6,000-year history has been revealed for the first time. This true knowledge of them is causing trembling and fear. They are today, more than in former days, reminded of the destruction of Noah's people and of the burning fall of Sodom and Gomorrah and of ancient Babylon.

The great destructive force of Allah's force against His enemies is known to the American scientists. My people have not the knowledge of self, kind, God, nor the Devil. They are the ones that the truth must come to. The knowledge of God and the Devil points out to us the way of escape. The devils could not tell you that they are the made enemies of the Black man, the opposers of peace and righteousness, the lovers of evil and haters of good. The secret of this people of actually being the devils was not to be revealed until they had lived their time of 6,000 years, which was up in 1914. Allah revealed them on His coming. He appeared under the name of Wallace Fard Muhammad in 1930. His work included the redemption of the so-called Negroes who are the Lost and Found members of the Black People.

We are the actual children of God and the members of the Family of God. We are the true owners of the earth which the devil was given the power to rule for the past 6,000 years. It is with praise and gratefulness that we should wait on the judgment of Allah. Once again, we will acquire the freedom to live and worship our Creator without the fear of the interference and disturbance of the devils. We should be thankful that the end of the wicked ruling power of this world is at hand.

We must realize that we, too, are taking part in the judgment, and we will be judged upon our acceptance of the Truth. We are today given a choice: all those, whose out of their own desire, choose to remain with your and God's open enemy (White Man), then let it be written, let it be done. Those who separate from the devils (the Caucasian race) in this day will be among the chosen of God and will inherit the New World, the Kingdom of everlasting life, as we read in the Bible.

As we further read in the Holy Qur'an, they will enter gardens beneath which rivers flow and where the greetings therein shall be. Peace! So, it comes to you as a warning of the time in which we now live, separation or death! It will mean death to both Black and White to integrate; it will mean death to White America to refuse to give up the Negroes.

The White man, I must repeat is talking integration today instead of separation because he sees "Lazarus" (the Bible's symbolic character of the Negro) running to Abraham's bosom. He knows that he cannot get to a safe place to lay his head. They desire to carry as many of my people into hell fire with them as possible.

Hurry and join onto your own kind. The time of this world is at hand.

SEPARATION OR DEATH III

Separation of the two (so-called Negroes and Whites) is the only solution to the ever-growing problem of "What must be done with the Negroes?" Both the so-called Negroes and their white slave masters do not seem to want to let go of one another. While the separation of the two races would be an act of wisdom and justice, on the other hand, to force integration which means socializing and intermarrying of the two races would be an act of swallowing up of the so-called Negroes' race by the slave masters, or by mongrelizing the two races, will destroy the respect of the society of both, nationally and internationally. Again, integration is against the wishes of the intelligent thinking group of both races—they want to preserve their race and the respect of their society.

The government is trying to enforce this wicked and contrary law to the Divine law and plan of Allah (God), which will end in revolution and war and the total destruction of the wealth of America.

Integration is not the wise and proper way of solving the "so-called Negro problem in America," but is an outright deceitful and wicked plan to destroy the Divine Plan of Allah or the future of the so-called Negroes. Both are sure to run into trouble with Allah's chastisement as it is plainly hinted and written in the Holy Qur'an. (I will gladly point it out to the disputer.) The wise White scientists know it as well as I and hope to prevent it; but they are outnumbered by their wicked wise. Allah (God) created two kinds of everything, so it is with man. He did not intend for them (so-called Negroes and Whites) to mix. He (Allah) has set a day of reckoning for those who willfully and knowingly break His natural law in which He created man.

It is their purpose to try and make Allah a liar so as to deceive the blind, deaf and dumb so-called Negroes—just as the devil deceived Adam and Eve in the Garden of Paradise. While knowing fully well that they would lose their place with Allah and a peaceful home if they accepted his advice (Holy Qur'an

7:20, 21), so it will be with the so-called American Negroes who, after being offered heaven at once by Allah, accept the wicked advice and offers (not office) of a temporary enjoyment and racial intermarriage and having sexual intercourse with a people whom Allah is angry with. He will punish both parties as He did Israel and the people whom Jehovah (God) forbade Israel to have intercourse with. Israel was punished and finally lost the goal which Jehovah had set before her and the deceiving enemies of Israel were destroyed.

SEPARATION OR DEATH IV

Allah (God) offers we the Lost-Found members of the Nation of Islam (the so-called Negroes) heaven at once, if we would only submit and accept Him. He (Allah) has already accepted us, but due to blindness (mentally), fear and love for the devil slave masters and their children, put in them by the White devil slave masters over three hundred years ago, the Lost-Found Black people of America act like fools, though they may have college and university education. The White man's education, without the knowledge of him and your own self, will never remove your fear of the devil slave masters' children nor will it remove your desire and love to be like them (the devils).

The evil done to us by these White devils are unforgiveable—this the poor Black man should know, but he doesn't! They must be taught this vital truth, that there can never be a judgment of this world until this 20 million Lost-found people hear the TRUTH (the knowledge of self, God and the devil). The blindness of the Black clergy and politicians is pitiful. It is a shame they were made so dumb by the devils, that even today, the day of our salvation, the leaders are just as blind as their followers. Both are following the devils into the lake of fire.

It is very sorrowful to see and know how our people in the South and throughout America are begging the White people (their real open enemies, the devils) to accept them into their social equality, instead of asking for the opportunity to separate from them. The heads of this disgraceful program, seeking love and friendship of the devils, are the so-called leaders; Black preachers and Black politicians. The NAACP could be made a powerful organization if they would accept Islam, Allah and His Messenger, otherwise it will soon disintegrate. If the Negro leadership was only wise to the clock of time and the slave master's code of laws for their Black slaves, they would be as I—seeking separation and a home of our own; somewhere on the Planet Earth which our Father created for us and not for this race of devils.

This type of Christianity that the devils gave my people is taking them to hell instead of heaven. The true religion of God is Islam and others WILL NOT BE ACCEPTED. You must be freed and separated from the slave masters. The slave code of laws that the devil made for we the lost-found Nation of Islam, makes us a permanent piece of property, belonging to them. No power of self-redemption or change of masters. No access to the judiciary, no honest provision for testing the claims of the enslaved to freedom, rejection of testimony of so-called Negroes (regardless to the nature, true or false), or whether slaves or free.

The laws are unequal. Free social worship and religious instruction prohibited. The legal recognition of the Negroes' rights is ignored. Submission is required of all so-called Negroes to all White devils, as written in the slave code of laws, as enforced in many parts of the United States of America over Negroes and Indians, or any people of color. Adequate protection for the lost-founds (so-called Negroes) under the devil's _____ is almost impossible. All White devils are brothers and friends of each other against the Black people.

According to the American Slave Code of Law, by William Goodell—page 304, under the above title, the Negroes may be used as breeders, prostitutes, concubines, pimps, tapsters, attendants at the gaming table and as subjects of medical and surgical experiments for the benefit of science. The evil and worst part of it all is the fact that the devils, White people, destroyed the Negro's love for self and turned the Negro's love for self toward his enemies.

HURRY AND JOIN ONTO YOUR OWN KIND. THE TIME OF THIS WORLD IS AT HAND.

SEPARATION OR TROUBLE?

Separation of the two (Negro and White) is the only solution to the ever-growing problem of "What must be with the Negroes?" Both so-called Negroes and their White slave-masters do not seem to want to let go one another. While the separation of the two races would be an act of wisdom and justice, on the other hand, to force integration, which means socializing, intermarrying of the two races (Black and White) and the eventual swallowing up of the so-called Negroes' race by their White slave-masters, or mongrelizing the two races, this will destroy the respect of the society of both, nationally and internationally. Again, integration is against the wishes of the intelligent thinking group of both races—these want to preserve their race and the respect of their society.

The government is trying to enforce this wicked and contrary law to the Divine Law and place of God, which will end in revolution and war, and total destruction of the wealth of America. This integration is not the wise and proper way of solving so-called Negroes' problem in America but is an outright deceitful and wicked plan to destroy the Divine Plan of Allah for the future of the so-called Negroes. Both are sure to run into trouble with Allah's chastisement—both Negroes and Whites, as it is plainly hinted and written in the Bible and Holy Qur'an. (I will gladly put it out to the disputer).

The wise White scientists know it as well as I, and hope to prevent it, but they are outnumbered by their wicked wise. God created two kinds of everything, so it is with man. He didn't intend for them (Negro and White) to mix and has set a day of reckoning for those who will fully, and knowingly break His natural law in which He hast created man. It is their purpose to try and make Allah (God) a liar, so as to deceive the blind, deaf and dumb so-called Negroes, as the devil deceived Adam and Eve in the garden of Paradise. While knowing fully well that they would lose their place with Allah and a peaceful home if they accepted his advice, so it will be with the so-called

American Negroes, who are being offered heaven at once by Allah, accepts the wicked advice and the office of a temporary enjoyment with racial intermarrying and having sexual intercourse with a people with whom Allah is angry.

He will punish both parties as he did Israel and the people whom Jehovah forbid Israel to intercourse with. Israel was punished, and finally lost the goal which Jehovah had set before her and the deceiving enemies of Israel were destroyed. I warn you to let Israel's history, from the days of Moses to this day, be a lesson to you. REMEMBER, both Israel and the Christians are on the brink of a pit of fire. The best and only solution of this problem of the so-called Negroes is SEPARATION and give them a start in a territory to themselves, regardless to the ignorant love of the slave for his master.

Take a look at the foolish plan of Martin Luther King for the poor so-called Negroes and how he and his plan were criticized by Mr. James B. Kilpatrick, Saturday, on the Television program, "Nation's Future." There we saw the man, Rev. King, a college man, a Christian Minister and Pastor, with a plan to take our poor people and himself and throw them at the mercy of an angry Negro-hating mob, to be beaten and killed for nothing; only to be accepted as Whites accept White, in White private-owned places, and finally allow his people to become White, and to mongrelize both races.

What does he think the intelligent White and Black people think of his silly plan? What kind of foolish so-called Negro parents will let such foolish preachers use their babies as a test of the mob's fire? What will those children think of such parents when they grow up and see the light of truth? Mr. Kilpatrick asked Rev. King, "Why do you want to integrate and make your race a coffee color, with complete integration, losing your race identify?" He was telling Martin Luther King, in so many words, that you and your race will not cause the White race to lose their identity, but the Negro will lose his. Such slander and mockery coming to the decent and intelligent so-called Negro by the ignorant love of a so-called religious leader of his people is a disgrace.

Such short-sightedness by Rev. King and the NAACP for the so-called Negroes of America, is making the nations of the earth, both Black and White, laugh us to scorn, to see us, a race of lazy beggars, great lovers of our enemies, desire to destroy our race to become ONE in our enemies. Why doesn't Mr. King and his NAACP organization join with me on a decent plan; a plan that makes sense and one that will make a future for our people. Ask for separation and some of this good earth that we can call our own, where we can live in peace together, away from those who do not want us. This is the plan of God and it will bring an end to the ever-growing trouble between the two races. If the White man (some of them) wanted to colonize us in Central America back in 1867, why not a free territory today, for we will not accept colonization. It is the time of our FREEDOM, and we will not accept anything less.

The NAACP and Mr. King want the freedom of voting, and in this way, they think they will be able to gain equal power in a White man's government and country. A Negro will never be the president under the Stars and Stripes of America. If he did, what could he do but to bow to the wishes of the owners of the Stars and Stripes? Let us seek some stars for our own nation and stop begging the White man for that which he has. We are not in such condition as being at the mercy of the White race, as long as we are members of the Asiatic Nation.

Everyone that reads this article, cut it out and show it to your friends; buy, or make your subscription to this paper now!

HURRY AND JOIN ONTO YOUR OWN. THE TIME OF

SEPARATION SOLVES THE PROBLEM

THERE IS NO DOUBT THAT we are living in the time of universal separation of Black and White. Due to your ignorance of the time, and the Divine Plans of Allah (God), you probably would not like to hear or talk about it. The wise and alert people of yours have knowledge of it, but do not like to talk it because of the love they have for the present world. The poor, ignorant ones have no knowledge of it, and care less as long as they are given the crumbs. It is not your will or power which is bringing it about. It is the Will and Power of Allah (God) as foretold by His Prophets from Moses to Muhammad.

How many of my people, the Lost-Found members of the Asiatic Nation (the (so-called Negroes) know that this is the Bible's judgement of this world and that the Divine Truth of Allah (God) is that which separates the righteous from the wicked? You may ask, "Who are the wicked?" The wicked are the people who were created wicked by nature (the Caucasian Race) whose limited time was 6,000 years. They have many followers of all races of earth—Black, Brown, Yellow and Red—but this does not mean that the Black Nations are wicked by nature. They are righteous, by nature, who are the real original people and owners of the earth.

The White or Caucasian (European) race is known to God and His Prophets as Satan, the Devil, the Enemy of God, and the enemy of His People (the Original Nation). Power was given to them to rule, with evil and falsehood, the darker Nations for 6,000 years. This they have done, and are now 46 years overtime, and they know this. It will take a few years to complete the separation, but nevertheless, the work is going on now at a very good rate of speed.

Search the history of these people (Black and White). The two have never been able to live in peace together. The White race is, as the Bible says of them, under the symbol of a troubled sea (Isaiah 57:20), never at peace and is the hater of truth and righteousness. The so-called Negroes know them and their evil doings better than any people but being without a teacher of their own kind or the past 400 years, they have become such lovers and great admirers of the devils and their evil doings that they do not want to be separated. That is why the problem is so hard to solve though the work will be done regardless to whom or what.

We number over seventeen million here in America and are without a home of our own, and a true friend, unless it is Allah. The wicked must be punished for their wickedness poured upon us without ever being hindered. This country is large enough to separate the two (Black and White). They can live here, but that would not be successful. The best solution is for everyone to go to his own people and country. We, the so-called Negroes, have both a great Nation to go to and a great country. Allah (God) has come for our return. The native home of the White race is Europe. It is up to you and me to obey the Word of Allah (God) or obey our own desire. This is for the sake of saving your own flesh and blood from the destruction of this evil, murderous race who is ever seeking an excuse to take your innocent lives, and to cut you off from good. They are ever around and in your homes after your girls and women to make you a disgrace before God and your people. YOU MUST JOIN ONTO YOUR OWN KIND. You may hate me now but one day you will love me.

Think it over: Why should we believe in their religion? Why should we be called by our enemies' names who enslaved our parents and will not give us equal justice, since we are free to choose our own people's names? Why should we continue to make fools of ourselves and our children begging them to accept us as their people when we have a Great nation to turn to? Hurry and join onto your own kind. The time of this world is at hand.

SOME OF THIS EARTH

Listen brothers, regardless to your profession or trade, or you may be the poor in the mud, agree with me on common sense. We are a nation (20,000,000) in a nation. What do you see of good in the future for us, that is, being subjected to the children of our father's slave masters? The children of the slave masters have the same mind of their fathers – full of hatred and murder (death) for you and I.

You are ever deprived of equal justice and opportunity. You are at the mercy of a four hundred-year-old open enemy, who has deceived you ever since you have been in the western hemisphere. They have given us a picture of their bloody hatred of our black, brown, yellow and red races. They divide, rob, rule and hold out false promises to all – they have swollen us up with these promises.

Where do you see any hope of a good future in our open enemies, for our sons and daughters? Are you depending on being a servant forever for them? Suppose the nations of earth push them out of their countries and cut off trade with this people. Will there be jobs enough for them and you, who number 20,000,000? Self-preservation is the first law of nature. Both nations (black and white) birthrates are ever-increasing. Your hope of survival is in the mercy of your enemies to provide employment for you and your children, or some soup and bread.

With educated people and scientists of our own, don't you think we are universally foolish people? We have no unity, no love of self, and no desire to be self-independent, which is due to laziness. Some of our people think the Christian religion is sufficient – this the enemy has been successful in deceiving you. Actually, the Christians and their religion, as you know it will not see the hereafter.

We the Muslims, under the Guidance of Allah, will rule forever. We are the righteous, the wisest and the powerful, in which whatever is in the heavens and earth, obeys. Without some of this good earth, that we can call our own, it would be better that we all commit suicide. Come unite with me and my God, Allah, and you will get what you want (heaven in this life). My followers and I are an example of love and unity. We are the people of Allah (God) and are guided and protected by Him, to Whom all praises are due forever.

A Muslim can live here or there. We will never be slaves anymore. Death is better than being a permanent servant to such enemies that you and I are subjected to. Come unite with me and my God, Allah, and get some of this earth for ourselves and children or die in the attempt.

HURRY AND JOIN ONTO YOUR OWN KIND. THE TIME OF THIS WORLD IS AT HAND.

SOME OF THIS GOOD EARTH THAT WE CAN CALL OUR OWN

Stop wasting your money! Your money was not given to you and it came the hard way, so why should you give it away for that which you can do without? If you and I would do just that, we could save millions of dollars which we could put into education, the purchasing of land, machines, poultry, milk cows, beef cattle, sheep, machines to cultivate the land to cut and saw timber to build homes for ourselves. We should dig for mud to mold and burn into bricks for our own homes and factories and grow our own cotton to make the clothes which we wear. We should feed our own stomach and hire our own scientists from among ourselves. Produce your own needs and capture our own market before it is too late.

How can we begin? Stop spending money for tobacco, dope, cigarettes, whiskey, wine beer, fine clothes, fine automobiles, fine furniture, expensive rugs and carpets, gambling, prostitution, idleness, sport and play, games of chance and horse racing. Stop careless spending of money, credits, loans at a high interest, which means selling yourselves to slave for the "loan sharks." Stop going into stores seeking the highest priced merchandise to purchase. Buy according to your means (your income). If your income is only $75.00 or $100.00 per week, and your rent is about the same every month, and food about the same price; and you have clothes, transportation and other little bills to pay, can you then afford a high-priced car note of $100 to $145 per month? If you must have a car, buy the low-priced car, or a rich man's used car; and not his used Cadillacs and Rolls Royce. I hope that you will begin leaving off the use of these things which you do not need to buy.

For your health's sake, stop eating the swine's flesh (the animal that was grafted from cat, rat and dog for medical purposes, and said to be nine hundred and ninety-nine percent poison! Live and act as a civilized person and we will soon be able to say that we are living like civilized people, along with love and unity in the Name of your God and religion, Islam.

If you will write to The Public Relations Department, Muhammad's Mosque No. 2, Chicago, Illinois, we will send you information on how we can help build a great future for the so-called Negroes in America by just sacrificing the money that we throw away to destroy our health in cigarettes, beer, wine, hog and whiskey for one week out of each month!

Allah (God) does not like, for us to break His law by eating the swine's flesh, drinking intoxicating drinks and using the poison tobacco weed. We must make a better future for ourselves and our children. Stop wasting and spending our money with the rich and spend it among ourselves, for we are the poor. Stop walking past your own Black brother's business to buy the merchandise of the rich just because the rich can sell at a lower price than your poor brother. Trade with your own kind until you are able to compete in prices.

HURRY AND JOIN ONTO YOUR OWN KIND. THE TIME OF THIS WORLD IS AT HAND.

THE BLINDNESS OF NEGRO PREACHERS

Allah (God) has brought to us the light of Truth. This light, the devils (White race) hope to put out with the help of the mentally blind, deaf and dumb Negro Preachers. Just as Pharaoh thought he would be able to put out the light of Allah (Jehovah), that He kindled in Israel through His servant Moses, with the help of his spiritually blind magicians (preachers). But they met with Musa (Moses), Allah's servant, there, the false light of the magicians was put out by the true light of Allah (Jehovah).

This king had no love for Israel, just as the President of America and the American citizens have no love for their so-called Negroes. Pharaoh was afraid of the light that was kindled in Israel by Allah (Jehovah), through His servant Musa (Moses) so that he became angry. He began to plan the death of Musa and the future of Israel by killing off the male babies of Israel. He was afraid, says the Holy Qur'an, that the light of truth preached by Musa (Moses) would change Israel's beliefs in Pharaoh's false religion, which he had made Israel to believe.

So, it is with this modern Egypt (America) and its rulers and people. They know they have blinded the poor so-called Negroes to the knowledge of truth. They pose as Divine representatives to the Black man; while at the same time, being the real devils, leading the Negroes away from the true God and true religion into a false religion. They mislead them under the name of a true prophet of Allah, named Jesus. These devil-made and handpicked leaders and preachers of our poor people, the devils have made to help crush and put out the real light of truth revealed to me from Allah, in the person of Master Fard Muhammad.

He (Allah) is the Negroes' long-awaited Jesus Christ, our Saviour and Deliverer, and the Crusher of our enemies (the devils.) It was made manifest how rotten, blind and fearful the devil-made preachers are, on September 10, 1961, at Griffith

Stadium, in Washington, D.C., on the subject: "Christianity vs. Islam." There Elder Lightfoot Solomon Michaux made no attempts to challenge the truth that I used in condemning Christianity as a Divinely revealed religion. And no attempts to challenge me that Jesus was not the founder of the religion of Christianity; that he (Jesus) was only a prophet, as Moses and the Prophets that followed in history after Moses, and Jesus was not the Christ. He wasn't the Son of God any more than any other righteous original man. It is false and wrong to accuse God of getting a son out of wedlock, and it is false to believe that God is a spirit, while all of God's people are made of flesh and blood.

In secret, this Elder Michaux had agreed at my home that Thursday before the 10th of September, that he believed in what I was teaching and that he believed the White man to be the devil. But when he spoke behind me that Sunday, there were devils sitting in the meeting and he, Michaux, wanted their friendship so he turned to them and shouted, "I love White people." Such double-crossing, hypocriting preachers cannot be trusted with good leadership for their already blind, deaf and dumb people.

According to some newspapers and magazines, Reverend Martin Luther King says that he doesn't like the Black Muslim's basic beliefs—Black Supremacy. Because, he says, Black Supremacy is as bad as White Supremacy. Reverend King, in such words, makes himself either neutral or a hypocrite on both sides—the Black and White nation; due to his fear of the devils. The Negro preachers never speak, actually, the truth of what is in them. He speaks the way he thinks will please the White devils. He cares not for the friendship of God and his people, (the so-called Negroes). He is after the friendship of the enemies of God and His people, (the American Whites).

Reverend Martin King is very lucky to have one Negro following him, who openly tells the poor, downtrodden Black people in words, that he never wants to see or live under the supreme rulership of the Black Nation—for they would be just as bad as White Supremacy! He has never lived under his own people's rule. He never has seen the Black man lynching and burning the Black man. He never had the experience of having to go on freedom rides, sit-in strikes under Black rule, to force them to serve him. Mr. King and his followers are showing the world that they love White Supremacy and hope it will rule them forever.

Reverend Martin Luther King is not trying to teach and make the lazy, White lovers, who are followers of his to unite and do something for self. But rather, he is aiding them to never have a desire to do for self. But to live by begging the White man to share his wealth with the Negroes and force the White people to share in everything that the White man has and not to worry about doing for self.

This is the worst teaching I have ever heard of in this modern day, of the rise of the Black Nation. The Reverend King would not be able to live where the Black man is going after something for self. The scared, rotten, White-poisoned preachers should be driven to the rear of the people until they learn that we, the Black Nation, the First and the Last, under the Guidance of Allah, will rule successfully our own selves—without the help of these devils. STOP depending on OTHERS and help SELF! Unite and seek a place on this earth that you can call your own as other Nations. Stop seeking the love and recognition of the devils.

Hurry and join onto your own kind. The time of this world is at hand!

THE COMING OF THE SON OF MAN

"And then shall appear the sign of the Son of man in heaven; and then shall all the tribes of the earth mourn, and they shall see the Son of man coming in the clouds of heaven with power and great glory." Matthew 24:30. Here in the plainest words is the Son of man on the Judgement Day. We are not told by either Moses or Jesus to look for God on the Judgement Day to be anything other than man. Spirits and spooks cannot be the judge of man's affairs. Man is material of the earth. How long will you be ignorant of the reality of God? You are poisoned by the devil's touch.

Why are you looking for a God that is not in flesh and blood as you are? Spirits can only be found in another being like yourself. What pleasure would you have in an invisible world? And on the other hand, what pleasure would spirits have in this material universe of ours? Your very nature is against your being anything other than a human being.

These are the days of the resurrection of the mentally dead so-called Negroes. The Son of man is here. His coming has been fulfilled. He seeks that which was lost (the so-called Negroes). Many are now receiving His name, and that name alone will save you. The wicked nations of the earth are sorry and angry to see the Son of man set up a government of justice and peace over this, their wicked and unjust world. They see His signs of great power to execute Judgment on the world of the wicked, in the heavens (sky), and they mourn.

We must have a new ruler, and a new government, where the people can enjoy freedom, justice, and equality. Let the so-called Negroes rejoice, for Allah has prepared for them, what the eye has not seen, the ear has not heard and that which the heart has not been able to conceive. The enemy knows this to be true and is now doing everything to prevent the so-called Negroes from seeing the hereafter.

HURRY AND JOIN UNTO YOUR OWN KIND. THE TIME OF THIS WORLD IS AT HAND

THE DOOM

It is for forbidden for the righteous to have friendly relations with the wicked, who are the enemies of God, His Prophets, His Scriptures, and His Religion of Peace, ISLAM. "O you who believe, take not my enemy and your enemy for friends. Would you offer them love, while they deny the TRUTH that has come to you? Driving out The Messenger and yourselves because you believe in Allah, your Lord! If you have come forth to strive in My Way and to seek My Pleasure, would you love them in secret? And I know what you conceal and what you manifest. And whoever of you that does this, he indeed strays from the straight path. If they overcome you, they will be your enemies, and will stretch forth their hand and their tongues towards you with evil: and they desire that you may disbelieve." (Holy Qur'an 60:1, 2)

My people, the TRUTH (Islam) has come to you, why not believe? It is because you are guilty of loving your enemies, and the enemies of Allah (God), His Messengers, His Prophets and His Religion? Allah has made manifest to you, His enemies, the White race. They are His enemies, your enemies, the enemies of our fathers, and our nation; the black, brown, yellow and red man.

The poor NAACP Black leaders, who are yet blind, deaf and dumb, are in love with these open enemies of Allah (God) and their own people, the so-called Negroes. The so-called Black leaders are against separation from these universally known enemies of the Black nation due to their open and secret love of membership in the White race and a position as a permanent servant in their house and country. These are the same enemies who forced our forefathers into servitude slavery for 300 years, and still own them as their property.

The (NAACP leaders) boast that they have equal rights with the master in the U.S.A. Whatever is the master's it is also the slave's. They believe the master should beat and kill his brothers to enforce equal rights between the slave and the master—what a foolish people! They think that they, not the White race can live without each other and therefore should not be separated. It is an open and universal fool who loves his enemies and the enemies of his God and people.

Ask these dumb leaders, who is it that deprives them of freedom, justice and equality? They will say the White man. Ask them who was it that enslaved you, lynched, burned, beat and killed you out of the law of justice all over America? They will say the White man. Ask them who killed God's Prophets and crucified Jesus? They will say, the White man. Ask them who was it that started the war in Europe and in the 30's, and on Ethiopia? Was it the Black nation (Islam) or the White race (Christianity)? They will say the White man. Then ask them, does not your bible teach "whosoever therefore will be a friend of the world (the White race is the ruler of the world) is the enemy of God? (James 4:4) They will say yes. Then ask them, have you not heard that Allah has revealed to His Servant (Elijah Muhammad) that this is a race of devils and that by nature they cannot love justice and righteousness? They will say yes.

Then say, O foolish of all the people, why not believe and seek your God and people like yourselves? Did not they (the White race) stretch forth their hands and tongue against Martin Luther King and his followers in the South, when he tried to force the White brothers against each other to enforce the law of integration—a law which would mongrelize the White and Black people? Yes, but you yet love the enemies of Allah (God) and yourselves; so, wait and see who will be happy and who will be unhappy.

HURRY AND JOIN ONTO YOUR OWN KIND. THE TIME OF THIS WORLD IS AT HAND.

THE DOOM DRAWS NEAR

"And affliction is combined with affliction. To thy Lord on that day is the driving" (Holy Qur'an 75:29, 30)

A rich and powerful people living in luxury, having everything that their souls desire. Feeling secure from harm coming to them because of their strong and powerful fortifications, and well-trained, well-fed armies. Having armed planes and ships carrying death to one another; stock piles of bombs of death waiting for the hour to be released on the nations. No peace, no safety in such a world that you and I are now living in.

The people of Allah (the so-called Negroes), are mentally dead to this time, as the people were in the days when Moses was sent to Pharaoh to bring Israel out of the bondage of the Egyptians, into a land where they could enjoy self-independence. Instead of them (Israelites) being happy to hear that God was ready to deliver them from Pharaoh, and to give them a goodly land, they set to contend with Moses and to help Pharaoh oppose Moses and Jehovah. They knew not that they were fighting a losing battle, until Jehovah began plaguing Egypt. With armies that the Egyptian armies were helpless to fight, Jehovah brought both Israel and Pharaoh to their knees, in submission. As the Bible's second book (Exodus) opens with war over a chosen people, it closes also with war for another people. Pharaoh was drowned in the Red Sea and the Beast destroyed in a lake of fire.

America is more guilty of mistreating the people of God (the so-called Negroes), than Pharaoh or any slave masters that recorded history makes mention of. The doom of America is at her door. This is the Great Judgment of the most powerful nation on earth, of the White race, but she is the most wicked of all. America will not do justice by her slaves (the so-called Negroes). She claims they are free but is aware of the fact that they are mentally enslaved and by no means know how to go for self.

America has always mistreated the so-called Negroes by beating and killing them to put fear in the others; shooting them down in the streets and highways for little of nothing. She (America) takes her slaves to be her worst enemies. She has never treated any enemy that she has warred with, as she has and still treats, her harmless slaves. They have made the Negro to even love them and have them killing their brother-slave to satisfy the blood-thirsty, merciless masters.

Allah has now chosen the poor Negroes to be His people and will slay you as He did Pharaoh and many Kings and empires who were even stronger than you according to the Holy Qur'an and the remains of their civilizations are found under the sand in Egypt and Arabia. Affliction upon affliction shall come upon you. Dust storms, hail storms and other destructive storms have served as a reminder for America, that Allah (God) is after her. Now if droughts and earthquakes follow, you should not be surprised. You must give up the so-called Negroes to meet their God and live on some of this earth that they can call their own.

HURRY AND JOIN ONTO YOUR OWN KIND. THE TIME OF THIS WORLD IS AT HAND.

THE END

We are fulfilling that which is written of us in the scriptures (Which we must read: Matthew 5:11; 10:23; 23:34; Revelation 12:13.)

My followers and I do not belong to the slave masters anymore. We belong to Allah (God) in whose name we are called; this is universally known. But as it is written: "You will be persecuted until the help of Allah comes." (Holy Qur'an) That help is very near.

America's jails, I was told, are filled. Some of them are so overcrowded that many of the prisoners have to sleep in the hallways. But, yet, she (America) rejoices in persecuting the Muslims under false charges, just to discourage our poor, blind, deaf and dumb people from accepting the truth (Islam) and returning to their true God, Allah, and His true religion, Islam.

PREY TO GOVERNMENT

We, the original people, are a prey to the government of America. Who must now be freed and separated from our enemies, the slave masters and their children if we are to ever enjoy peace, freedom, justice and equality.

Twenty million of our people cannot depend on another nation for existence. We must look to God and self as other nations had to do, or continue to beg our enemies (White slave masters) for jobs to exist among them, instead of asking and demanding a chance to go for self, to create our own jobs.

This is a disgrace to the leadership of 20 million people who do not want the responsibility of caring for self. Well, the time is very near when you'll have to go for self.

SOMETHING OF PAST

America's and the entire White race's ruling power over the brown, red, yellow and black nations of Africa and Asia will soon be something of the past. No longer will these nations bow to the Western powers. America's DOOM is sealed, and is inevitable, according to the word of Allah (God) to me.

Allah desires to make Himself known to the world, that He alone is God and has appeared among us in the Person of Master W. Fard Muhammad.

____ Bible and Qur'an teaches of the presence of God in person at the end of the world of Satan and the devil's rule. We would be foolish to disbelieve that such character is not present and is not directing the course of the nations today.

ALLAH AGAINST WHITES

The American White race is the number one people whom Allah's anger is directed against as Jehovah's anger was against Egypt in the time of Moses. Jehovah's weapons of war used against Pharaoh and His people were the forces of nature: flies, frogs, lice, diseases, rains, hailstones, fire, water and finally the drowning of Pharaoh and his armies in the Red Sea.

The same forces of nature are prepared to be used against America with the following additions: terrifying storms (which now harass America); the loss of friendship of the nations; a specially prepared enemy people under the name "Gog" and "Magog," whose skill and power will cover the earth for a while; there will be no friends for America; snow, ice and earthquakes, even droughts and dust storms, the natural powers of water, wind, terrific cold out of the north, fire from the sun, agitation of the high seas by the magnetism of the moon and sun which will aid in the destruction of America's sea power

SINS ARE GREATEST

This is referred to in the prophecy of Jesus: Read: Luke 21:25, also Isaiah 27:1, Revelation 8:7, 8, 9. America's sins are the greatest! Her sins are even worse than all the nations of the Earth combined. She sees and knows her doom is near.

She seeks to trick her slaves (so called Negroes) to share this doom with her. But she knows that her once slaves have a chance of escaping so she hypocritically offers them social equality under the name "integration," which she knows the blind, deaf and dumb will fall for, while it is an open trap of death for both sides.

My people do not realize this, nor will they believe this until they are hurt, or it is too late, or that this is the end of Satan's world, (power over the Black Nation of Islam) and must be told in the plainest language.

This is the work of Allah, not you and I. Read your Bible and Holy Qur'an. America has always hated and mistreated her slaves (so-called Negroes). Today, she backs up the police departments throughout the country to beat and kill poor Black men and women.

We have always been submissive to these cruel, merciless enemies—like lambs are to a pack of hungry wolves. Stop tricking your slaves, White America, separate them into a good place on some of this soil, that you robbed our people of, with superior weapons and supply them with that which is necessary to get started for self.

Then, maybe your doom will be delayed a while. Otherwise, Allah will do it and will not leave a place for you anywhere on the planet.

It is not the evil done to others by the White race of America; it is the unjustified evils done to the helpless Black slaves of America. Allah wishes to make America an example of His judgment that both Europe and Asia may know that He alone is God and has redeemed the helpless Black slaves from their merciless enemies. I have warned you! Take it or leave it!

Hurry and join onto your own kind. The time of this world is at hand!

THE GREAT DECEIVER

THE GREAT DECEIVERS

Arthur R. Gottschalk, State Senator, 8th District, Chicago, Park Forest, Ill., wrote our National Secretary, John Ali, asking him and my followers to disavow and repudiate publicly the truth Allah revealed to me of the Caucasian race; the truth of them being REAL DEVILS and our (the black Nation's) open enemies.

A part of the letter was printed and published in the Chicago Tribune, June 15th, 1962. The Senator, Gottschalk, failed to include in his letter to Secretary Ali, proof or material that the truth Allah has given me of them being real devils, is false. This leaves my secretary and followers helpless to deny the truth.

FAILED TO CONSULT MESSENGER

I am surprised at the intelligent Senator writing a letter before first making an attempt to consult me of what Allah has revealed to me. The Senator's letter is a perfect insult to my followers. Without showing proof of what I am teaching IS NOT the truth, he is asking my followers not to believe it, and tell the public that they do not believe.

What the Senator does not like is that my followers believe that the Caucasians (the white European race), are the real devils as Allah has said; also, the true history and teachings of the Prophets and their scripture (Bible and Holy Qur'an) bear witness.

I think the Senator has attacked something that may surprise him and his race because of his intentions of making my followers disbelieve in the truth of Allah as taught to me.

One of the characteristics of the devil is to deceive. In the last two paragraphs of his letter to our Secretary, John Ali, Gottschalk hoped to deceive him with the following words:

WORDS OF DECEPTION

"At this time, when men of good will of all races are working hard to promote harmonious human relations and eliminate the social and economic conditions which has produced injustices, it is tragic that men like Elijah Muhammad are attempting to tear down their good work and accentuate racial tension and misunderstanding."

Mr. Gottschalk, we are not your slaves anymore; therefore, do not misunderstand us. We care very little about you or anyone or races who would think, after the knowledge of you, that a promise of promoting harmonious human relations, social equality with you will solve our problem. You are mistaken! We want nothing less than freedom to build our own economy and society, and on some of this earth that we can call our own!

We want to be independent as you and other nations are, to do what we think is best for our own selves. What kind of future can you prepare for us other than subject slaves to you and your kind? I am not attempting to tear down anything good, for I have not found anything of good that you or your kind of have set up to tear down that was good for my people. Allah and I are the only one I know who are setting up any good work for our people.

LET US ENJOY FREEDOM

Since our government declares us to be free, why not leave us to go and enjoy this freedom to ourselves on some of this earth that we can call our own? The language used in your letter is that of a deceiver, who knows that he has laid hands upon a great value and hopes to deceive him to believe that, that which he has been given or found is of no value and what you have is the best.

The entire 20 or more million of my people here should learn a lesson from your letter, and be careful of you and your kind, corrupted promises of social equality without some of this earth we can call our own.

Your dogs enjoy honor in your society; they are seen eating from the table and riding in the same seat in some of your best transportation.

We do not desire any such place and level with all the evil you have done to us for the past 400 years and you continue to mistreat us.

IN FOR GREAT SURPRISE

Do you think we will be satisfied to settle with less than some of this earth we can call our own? I think you are in for a great surprise. The Senator is outright asking my followers to recant and make it publicly know that they disbelieve in the Truth Allah has revealed to me in the closing line of his letter to Secretary Ali in the follow words:

"I call upon you, John Ali, as National Secretary of your organization to disavow and repudiate publicly all of the above statements that the Caucasian race is a race of devils says Allah to me, by leader, Elijah Muhammad.

"Failure to do so would be a clear admission that the statements of Elijah Muhammad accurately represents the policy of your organization which sponsors and operates the University of Islam."

For nearly 32 years the students of our school have been in the knowledge of you and good reason of being at peace in your midst. This comes from having the knowledge of you. If you fear this true knowledge of yourself will cause your mistreated, once slaves to hate you, then your argument is with Almighty Allah who has revealed it. It is surely not with brother John Ali and my followers, for you will not be able to get them to give up the truth of you, their God, Allah, and their Leader and Teacher.

THE SO-CALLED NEGRO LEADERSHIP

The leadership of my people, the so-called American Negro, has absolutely aided the slave-master in keeping us a **subjected people.** The leadership continues to make a cry for social equality with White people. What intelligent people would want to **fraternize, intermingle, integrate, sweetheart and marry the kidnappers, murderers, enslavers and burners of their people?** Only a people such **as my people with blind leadership** would even desire or strive for such **a lowly disgraceful act!** The blind cannot lead the blind. The leaders of my people want and show great favor with the slave-master against the good of their own people.

The so-called **Negro editors, preachers, lawyers** and other **professional leaders** of our people continue to lead the fight in begging the White man for **civil rights.** History shows we have been in this part of the world for more than four hundred years. We served more than three hundred of those years in **servitude slavery.** We have been so-called free for one hundred years since we were freed, we have been called citizens of America. Why then are we seeking civil rights if we are **citizens of America?**

Why should the leaders of our people continue to beg the government to grant us civil rights? We don't have to beg the government to give us those glorious benefits that are laid down in the Constitution **in the 13th and 14th** Amendments. **If we are citizens**, we should be **enjoying them without asking for them!** Yet, we are still begging for justice! **You need a better leadership.**

The preacher leadership of my people are in the most **ignorant class.** They knowingly lead our people to a **path of destruction** and **disaster because of their love for and fear** of the enslavers of their people. We have records of several so-called Negro preachers who have made attempts to attack and destroy the Muslims and myself, The Messenger of Allah.

Reverend Borders of Atlanta, Georgia, on April 9, went on the air and stated to a radio audience that he would **drive the Muslims from the city of Atlanta** if he had **the people with him. Reverend Borders** would have an easier task of trying to dry the oceans up rather than direct his slave-masters slave-keeping attacks at us. Another preacher in **Monroe, Louisiana,** said the **White officers** who broke into our **religious service March 5,** on an **unarmed people, should have killed us!** This **ignorant preacher,** eager **to show his slave-master** that he is not with us, calls for the defeat of his own people.

Reverend **Gardner C. Taylor,** who is warring with **Reverend Jackson for control in the White man's Baptist religion,** chose the occasion again to denounce the Muslims who **practice Islam,** the religion of Almighty God Allah. The preachers claim that they are men of God. **Where is their proof?** It was the preachers who condemned Jesus to his death! **It was the elders who opposed Moses!** It has always been the **clergy class** who opposed the **prophets of God.**

Yes, the Scribes and Pharisees as they are referred to in the scriptures, have always opposed the righteous men of Allah. They oppose me today. The religious leaders of our people will soon learn they cannot overcome the purpose of God. In the **61st Surah of the Holy Qur'an,** it states that they desire to put out the word of Allah with their mouth.

The so-called Negro leadership does not care to give their own people justice as long as the White man does not. The Negro leadership and the slave-masters are as two murderers and thieves of my people. The White man murders us as the Negro leaders rob us. In fact, both will rob us.

Since our being **kidnapped** and brought to **America,** we have received nothing but promises. It is promises which today, satisfy the leaders of my people. There is the promise of fair **employment** and **integration** of **social mixing.** The devil is full of **tricks** and we cannot put any confidence in him.

The leaders of my people must remember that we are all Black people of the Black nation. **The hurt of one member** should be the **hurt of all of us**. Regardless of the type of leader for my people, he should not be afraid to speak for his brother. Regardless to where he may be, the leader should be for his brother. He should not flinch. My people must wake up and know their present leaders have failed them. Such leadership should and must be discarded!

The religion of Islam has powerful life-giving effects on the believers. Islam makes the believer feel that he should get up and begin doing something for self. Islam makes you and I see each other as brothers. Islam arouses the old love for each other that was put asleep in us by the slave-master. **I represent Islam as a religion to you.** I want you to know the power and effect of that religion on us. **If you ever accept Islam,** you will stand up as one people and a nation. You will not lay as a race of slaves! We have a God with us! He is not to come because He is already here. Many Christians will admit that God must be present among us. Some of us today in this vast, moving world do not even take a moment of time to think or even check to see if this is the day of God's visit to a people or if it is the day of the devil's visit.

I have been sent directly from Almighty God, whose proper Name is Allah. He has given me that which the prophets wrote of, which will give my people life. It will bring light to you and your understanding will return. The leadership of my people would be wise in joining with me in this Divine awakening of our people. Their interference will lead only to their destruction in a lake of fire with the enemy of their people.

HURRY AND JOIN ONTO YOUR OWN KIND. THE TIME OF THIS WORLD IS AT HAND.

THE SO-CALLED NEGRO LEADERSHIP II

Why do you oppose Freedom, Justice and Equality for your people and self? Freedom, indeed has not been given to you in America; no equal justice has come to you, nor equal opportunity. Should not the Leadership seek good for his people, even at the cost of his life? What future do we have in being integrated in the White race who are the children of those who enslaved our fathers and mothers? Daily, we live under the very shadow of death at the hands of their children.

We want for our 20 million people here in America, what White America has for herself. You are a Nation within a Nation, depending on White America for sole existence—without trying, or even seeking a chance to try and do something for self—other than to beg for that which belongs to White America. You beg as though you are too lazy to work and build a future for self. What future does 20 million no-Whites have in their slave-masters? Is not it clear to you that your hopes of existence depend only on whatever type of labor the White man will offer you? Can you hope to continue seeking employment for your 20 million people in the factories and offices of the White man, while he already has unemployment among his own which is increasing daily?

The ever-changing map of the White world is increasing their own problem of existence. You may be unable to see and foresee this, this is why we would like to help you see. Twenty million ex-slaves failing or refusing to see and go for self today, will prove to be fatal for them in the near future. If the blind cannot see his own way and refuses to be, led by the hand of the seeing one, who then can be sorry for his stumbles and falls?

Allah (God) is with us to do something for self, but you are opposed to doing something for self and choose to beg for the crumbs, while there are clear signs that soon there will be no crumbs for you. Judge between you and me in what I am seeking for our people and what you are seeking for them. I am seeking a permanent home for my people where they can be free to build a future for themselves. If you were only wise enough to come and confer with us, the picture would be a different one.

Gone forever is the Negro mule and plow. The White man is ever advancing in the science of machinery (mechanical devices) and is rapidly putting our people in the bread lines. Something must be done by us to check the spread of poverty, suffering and want of our people! We do not have to seek the solution. God has given it Himself. Submit to Allah, unite and let us go for self on some of this good earth.

You, as religious leaders of the people, are doing your people more harm than good in seeking to integrate them with the slave-master for total destruction. We must be separated from those who have enslaved us and are not willing to do Justice, nor grant us equal opportunity. WE MUST UNITE AND SEEK THESE THINGS FOR OURSELVES!

HURRY AND JOIN ONTO YOUR OWN KIND. THE TIME OF THIS WORLD IS AT HAND.

THE SO-CALLED NEGRO LEADERSHIP III

It is the Divine Will of Almighty God (Allah) that we be separated! It is very foolish on the part of so-called Negro leaders to oppose it! All of our opposition will be brought to naught! I am a man who preaches justice. I am not self-made, politically made, seeking office, nor am I in, a position because of wealth. I am Divinely sent! If Almighty God, Allah, were NOT with me, I could NOT get through America teaching, preaching and doing this Divine work. I want my people to be aware of this before the destruction takes place.

We need a place in the sun for the future of our people as other nations have and want. Our past leaders never asked for this. It was the same in the case of Moses. Moses demanded equal justice for Israel. The leaders opposed Moses in seeking freedom, justice and equality for his people. If you study the foolishness of the leaders of our people, you will agree that they are doing nothing but keeping our people bound in chains of slavery as beggars! Why don't the leaders demand something for their people? Why don't you unite and say "Give us some earth!" The black man should be interested in himself as the white man is interested in himself.

The leaders of my people should know you cannot compete with the white man as they are the owners and producers of the land. We can't be equal with the master until we have what the master has. We can become the equal and producers by securing land for our future as other nations. Land is needed not just for the Muslims and Elijah Muhammad, but for all of our people who have had nothing for their blood and labor during the more than 400 years that they have been in America. We need a place of our own to put our foot on. Why should the leaders of our people be like puppies begging for a crumb? We can't expect to make a future for twenty million people by lying around the white man's employment office. The white man, today, is having trouble creating and finding jobs for his OWN people! You will soon see, he offers YOU nothing but a promise.

Almighty God, Allah has for you, a promise of truth. No black man who has been beaten and trampled under foot of the slave master should reject the truth when it is presented. It is time for intellectuals, preachers and professional leaders to decide on something for the future of our people. The black man should demand something for himself. Unite with me and in the Name of Allah, we will get it! We have tried everything else, NOW try the TRUTH!

HURRY AND JOIN ONTO YOUR OWN KIND. THE TIME OF THIS WORLD IS AT HAND.

THE TRUTH

Often, I am asked: (1) How can we live separately from the White people in the same country? (2) How can we be independent of them? (3) Would the White Americans agree to a separate territory for us in some suitable area where we could go for self and live alone in peace? (4) Would we get along in peace with each other?

The first question is very easy to answer: The Black and White people, according to history, have always lived separately from each other. They were originally separated by God and the Law of God forbids their intermixing, or intermarrying. The earth was originally inhabited by the Black man.

FAMILIES TO THEMSELVES

Later on, as color (brown, yellow, red) began among them by the original scientists, (says the word of Allah to me) they became families to themselves, and from families to tribes; the term used today is "races" or "nations." Most of the Black remained in the East along and below the equator of the earth.

The White race, after their creation 6,000 years ago, was given the part of earth today that is called Europe.

It is this race of people who actually started the sin of intermixing the two strange bloods, which is forbidden by God; just as they have disregarded all Divine Laws of Allah (God). They even seem to change the very natural laws of man in which he is made.

They first mixed with the original Black Arabs, then, as they traveled over the earth, for the past near 500 years, they mixed with brown, yellow and red races. They captured the Blacks and made slaves of them. For the past 400 years, they have used them (so-called Negroes) for experimental purposes and even uses them now as one uses his tool!

HOW INDEPENDENCE IS BORN

The 2nd question: How can we be independent of the White race? Answer: When a people is smart enough to look and dig the earth and get what she produces, her secret treasures hidden under the surface, along with her water, air, and sunshine, that people can be self-supporting as other smart nations are, who are independent of each other.

Some may have in their part of the earth that which the other does not have; then comes the exchange of resources to others through peaceful means, a trade and exchange of goods with each nation.

I think the so-called Negroes and White Americans should have such restrictions and laws between them to maintain peace.

INTELLIGENT WILL AGREE

The 3rd question: Would White America agree to a separate territory for us, the Black, once slaves of the Americans? Answer: I do believe the intelligent minds of America would agree to the separation of us into some place other than trying to continue making us live with them with the same respect and justice that they enjoy—not to mention the mixing of bloods and the complete care of us. If they see you and me in honest togetherness on some of this earth that we can call our own, even with some help as Egypt did for Israel on Israel's departure, they will respect us.

The 4th question: Would we get along in peace if we were put together to live together? Answer: I know we would if our national religion would be ISLAM; this I am proving to you daily.

IT'S GOD IN ISLAM

See how peacefully my followers and I get along together? It is God in the religion of Islam who inspires love, unity and peace in the hearts and actions of every true believer. Once you accept

Islam, you do not even like to dispute and quarrel with the brothers or sisters. Allah will soon put Islam in the hearts of all the lost-found members of the Tribe of Shabazz.

Of course, there is that lost continent of Asia and Africa who will welcome every Lost-Found Muslim in America to share with them, if others fail. It is a MUST that we be separated into some part of this earth that we can call our own.

Next, do we have the qualified men and women among the Black people of America to run a government for self?

Only disagreement and war and fighting between each other would prevent such necessary union of Nations to get that from the other nations that she does not produce. A new nation should not isolate itself from national and international trade. However, this does not mean mixing blood with each other. The borders of a Black and White separate state should be as strict as any nation's borders, protected by passports and visas for all people.

TRUTH, PART II

The Sower of Truth is the Messenger or Apostle of Allah (God), but whose heart is fertile enough to germinate the Truth? In the same chapter Mark 4:23, it says: "If any man has ears to hear, let him hear." This was the great trouble Noah had with his people. They would not lend their ears to hear the truth and were therefore drowned by a flood of water. Lot had the same trouble with his people. They just would not listen to the Truth. It is the same today, as it was in the past. The people just will not hear the Truth. "Supremely exalted then is Allah, the King, the Truth" (Holy Qur'an 20:114).

AUTHOR OF THE TRUTH

Allah is the Author of the Truth. The heavens and the earth bear witness that Allah is the Author of Truth. Regardless to how small or great, all life bears witness to the Truth.

Since the heavens and the earth bear witness to the Truth of the existence of its Creator, falsehood cannot hope to gain a permanent place in the creation of truth. Darkness cannot find a permanent place because of forever being chased by light. So, it is with the devils, the fathers of falsehood.

They now seek a hiding place somewhere in the Creator's Creation of Truth (the universe) which cannot now be done. Falsehood vanishes in the light of Truth as darkness vanishes before light.

THE LIGHT OF TRUTH

Allah is the light of Truth in the Person of Master Fard Muhammad (the long-expected Mahdi or Messiah). His appearance in the World of Falsehood is like that of the sunrise against the night of darkness.

We have lived in a night of falsehood for six thousand years under the rule of Satan (the White race). This evil false rule must be removed by Allah to allow the real Nation of Truth to rule as they did before the night of falsehood. This is the time the change is being made. Today the Sun of Truth is casting her rays upon the dark Western horizon.

OUR UNITY DEMANDED

We the Darker People of the Western Hemisphere should unite and pull off our night garments and dress ourselves for today. Our unity is demanded. The original settlers (the Indians) of this Western Hemisphere and the Latin or Central American, must unite and accept their own.

The earth was created by the Black man, for the Black man and this is universally known by all scholars and scientists of religion.

The earth has been divided between four families (black, brown, red and yellow) for many thousands of years. The fifth family (the White race) was grafted in to be tried at ruling us, the Black nation. However, they have proven to be unworthy of keeping the peace and justice among us, the aboriginals.

Instead of peace, love and brotherhood, they have been successful in bringing about hell, dissatisfaction, and have made enemies between brother and brother (divided us one against the other).

WHITES MADE MISCHIEF

They have made mischief and caused bloodshed throughout the Nations of earth.

Now the nations that love peace and brotherhood are uniting behind our God of Peace and Justice to bring about the removal of this troublemaker, whom we have learned through experience, is disagreeable to live with in peace.

We should not hesitate to unite and take our place in our

own. What future do the so-called Negroes have under their 400-year-old enemies? Of all people, should not they unite and do something for self and stop depending on their open enemies for existence?

TRUTH, PART III

"O Apostle deliver what has been revealed to you from your Lord; and if you do it not, then you have not delivered His Message, and Allah will protect you from the people; surely Allah will not guide the unbelieving People." (Holy Qur'an 5:67)

When Allah (God) decides to reveal His Truth and bring an end to falsehood, that Truth must be delivered regardless of the cost! The Messenger of Truth should not fear to deliver it if that Truth is from Allah, He will be the Protector of it as well as the Protector of the Messenger who delivers it (Truth). A true Messenger of Allah never fears to deliver the Message of Allah, nor does he ever fail to deliver it—even though most of them (Messengers) and their followers suffered severe persecutions and even death; yet, the message of Allah was delivered.

The awakening of the Arabs nearly fourteen hundred years ago to the ancient Truth (Islam) (not a new Truth) of Allah by Muhammad and his work, was typical of what will be done today. He was opposed by the Arabs for a while. Although the Arab Nation and their country are the birthplace of the great prophets and Scriptures, and from there, prophets are sent throughout the world from the time of Adam until today, the Arab history cannot be compared with the history of the so-called Negroes who have never had a Divine prophet nor a Scripture!

According to the past histories of the major prophets, one comes every 2000 years until the end of the World of Sin. Moses came exactly two thousand years after Yakub (the God and Maker of the evil Caucasian race). Jesus came two thousand years after Moses, and the last prophet came two thousand years after Jesus, fulfilling much of the histories of the Prophets before him; especially Moses, David, Jesus and Muhammad. The man Allah (God) raised up from among the American so-called Negroes in the West will unite his people to Islam with the guidance of Allah with a book of Scripture for his people prepared and written by the fingers of Allah (God).

His teachings will be called a "New Islam" and will be opposed by many who would not like a change from the old to a higher knowledge of the Divine. The present Holy Qur'an Sharrieff leads us right up to the door of that final book for our future though not admitting us in; yet we are able to get a glance of some things.

The devil (White race) watches the Believers, and when he finds one showing any sign of weakness, he helps him to become more weaker in the faith. Islam is the greatest unifying force on the Planet Earth. Islam is a religion that is backed by the power of its Author, Allah, to Whom be praised forever. Islam could save the world from its destructive fall, but the world has practiced evil for so long that she would rather go to her doom than to turn and do righteousness. Look at the silly things the world is doing, working "like mad" to destroy each other! For what?

Is not there enough earth for every one of us? Yes, there is enough if we would be satisfied with our share, and not seek to rob the other man of his share. Billions upon billions of dollars are being spent for the purpose of destroying humanity from the face of the earth; which is nothing but a waste of money that could be spent for the happiness of the Nations and not for their wicked death. THE WICKED WILL BE THE LOSERS!

THE TRUTH IV

If there ever lived on this Planet Earth a people who deserved a part of it that they could call their own, it is you and me, the lost-found members of the Asiatic Nation from the tribe of Shabazz.

Today, Allah (God) offers you and me a chance to become the owners of some of His earth if we only submit to Him, I have submitted myself to Him and I am the first of the Lost-Found to submit to Him. Will you also submit to Him? We must have some of this earth for a home we can call our own as other nations.

20 MILLION IN U.S.

Twenty million of us here in America at the present time depend only on the White man for a job to survive. We are increasing in population daily. Do you ever take time to think for a moment, that twenty million non-Whites living and increasing in population among more than a hundred and twenty-five million Whites, whose parents our parents were slaves to? We have become a Nation in a Nation and one of us MUST live (separate) from the other in order to survive!

The present condition of the White race engulfs them in a universal war that will force them to look out for themselves only.

ANGRY AT EACH OTHER

All the nations are angry with each other, and Allah is angry with them. What kind of future do we have in such a mad world who have carved it up among themselves, but to submit to Allah (God) for a home? He (Allah) has said to me that He will set us in heaven at once if we would only submit to Him.

Do you not hear and read how the White race is killing your own Black people in Africa by the tens and hundreds of thousands?

They are killing them for no cause whatsoever, but to rule and rob them of their country's natural resources, and to enslave them with their false Christianity for cheap labor; just as they did our fathers here, and still have you in the status of a "free slave" with no hope but a job or the soup line. Yet, many of you glorify this same universal enemy enough to even integrate with them!

PAID FOR OUR HOME

We have paid well for a home on this soil with 400 years of shame. We have been disgraced, robbed of the knowledge of self and kind; we have sweated and bled for White America's riches, self-independence, security of property and lives. Will you not wake up and stand up to God and the Nations of the earth like a man of YOUR place and home on a part of this earth that you can call your own?

Do you feel proud representing yourselves under the White slave maker's names, and claiming what is theirs to be yours or partly yours? We need and must have something of our own, a home! Get out and farm! Raise the foods and clothes that you and your people must have! Get the earth, and build your own civilization of freedom, justice and equality.

You are the real "Lazarus" charmed by the riches of the slave masters and are too lazy to go for self! Some of you (so-called leaders) are well educated in the "know how," but would rather give your educational values back to your White teachers in their factories, plants, laboratories and offices; even to the extent of teaching their children. You even refer to the wealth and to this country of America as being "our wealth, our country," or "we," while at the same time you are begging for Civil Rights (which they will never give you).

HURRY and JOIN onto YOUR OWN KIND. THE TIME OF THIS WORLD IS AT HAND!

THE TRUTH V

SUBMIT TO ALLAH
(Holy Qur'an 2:12)

The power of all the religions of the world, other than Islam, are losing their attraction and power on the people of earth. Why? Number One (1): because they are too proud to submit to God according to the word of Allah (God) to me. It was not possible for the world to submit and believe in the religion of Islam before the end of the rule, and power of the devils (the White race). The White race (devils) was permitted to rule (Genesis 1:26) us not according to **Justice** and **Righteousness** but by evil and **falsehood**. They were made wise enough by their father **(Yakub)** to **deceive** us in making falsehood to appear to be true, until the time and appearance of the Author of Truth (Allah), and Justice. They (the White race) make evil appear to be very attractive (Genesis 3:6) and in this way they capture many of the righteous for unalike attracts.

MURDERERS BY NATURE

By nature, they are murderers and liars (Genesis 4:8; John 8:44), therefore, they could not believe (John 8:37-40) in a true religion like Islam which means man's entire Submission to the will of Allah (God).
Take a second look into the above said; if the devils were given the power to be the God of this world for a time (six thousand years), how could they by nature teach us to submit to Allah, and do the will of a God of Truth, freedom, justice and equality. Therefore, the people under a wicked ruler (the devil) of the world went astray from the True God and True Religion. They made for themselves all kinds of false gods and religions and bowed down and worshipped them.

THE TIME

Now is the time of the God of Truth and Justice to rule. The Black Nations are awakening to the knowledge of the time of our God (Allah) and are now seeking Him and His True religion called "Islam," to be united and live in peace together as they were before the creation of the White race (devils).

NEGRO PROGRESS SLOW

Islam was offered to this world by the Prophets of Allah (God), (see and read both the Bible and Holy Qur'an) but was unable to make their people believe in Islam (entire submission to the will of Allah (God). Moses, Jesus and Muhammad failed in their efforts to get this world to submit to the will of Allah (God), not to mention the many other lesser Prophets who spent their lifetime and efforts trying to convert the world; to submit to the will of Allah (God). Even today, due to the poison effect of the teachings of falsehood, the progress of truth and Justice among the so-called Negroes is very slow, to what it would be if there were no opposition by the enemies (devils). There are some White people better than others, but they are not to be mistaken for the righteous, because they are not as wicked as others of their kind.

One reason why the so-called Negroes reject Islam, because they don't know what it actually means, which is only entire submission to the will of Allah (God). As today, the people have submitted to do the will of the devils, not the will of the God of Truth and Justice (Allah).

Hurry and join onto your own kind. The time of this world is at hand.

THE TRUTH VI

"ISLAM"

The religion of Islam is now for the first time being offered to us, the so-called Negroes, the lost-found, and the lost members of the chosen nation by Allah (God) in person.

MOSLEM SHRINERS

Before the coming of Allah, Islam was sold to the so-called Negroes in a secret order or society called the Masons. This order is made up of thirty-three (33) degrees and it is sold by degrees. If a member is eligible and able to pay for all the degrees he may do so, but only those who take the thirty-third **(33rd)** are called **Moslem Shriners**.

Though real Islam is not practiced in this secret order, it is made a **farce**. The first three (3) degrees are the base of the whole, they are full of significance pertaining to the **robbery** and **murder** of a **valuable** member of a significant Temple, and a friend of the wisest King that ever lived.

ISLAM FREE

You do not have to buy Islam, it is free. Islam is the salvation of the Black Nation, and the only way out for the so-called American Negroes. Islam means submission to the will of Allah (God).

What greater religion than a religion that demands us to submit to the will of Almighty God (Allah)? The number one (1) principle of belief in Islam is the belief In **One God**. Is not this the teachings of the Prophets of old, **Abraham, Moses, Jesus,** and **Muhammad**?
Hurry and join unto your own kind. The time of this world is at hand.

THE TRUTH VII

Truth is that which is opposed to falsehood and the father of falsehood (the devil). The devils (white race) are opposed to truth and the author of truth, (the Divine Supreme Being). It is the plain Truth, only that is necessary to resurrect the mentally dead Black Nation.

God, in the Person of Master W.D. Fard Muhammad, the long-expected Messiah, the Muslims, Mahdi (Allah, God, in Person) has brought us this plain truth. The truth could not have come to us any sooner. It had to come from the mouth of Allah (God) in Person. He could not have brought it to us before this time.

HE HAD TO WAIT

He had to wait until the time given falsehood to rule had expired. Being afraid of the truth, because it is not in favor of the enemy of truth is absolutely inviting death and the eternal anger of Allah, God Almighty, whose purpose in coming is to rid the Black Nation once and for all of our chief enemy, the devil, the white race. This fear of the devils was put into our parents when they were babies, fear is even kept in us today by their beating and killing of our people without a cause.

FEAR is the real enemy that now stands between you and your salvation. The white man's strongest weapon which is FEAR is keeping us divided. FEAR is the enemy that keeps us divided and from becoming and independent people. It is at the height of ignorance for any educated black man or Nation to seek the continued dependence upon the enemy for their future. Especially, when the enemy has no future for self! John 8:32 says: "Ye shall know the truth."

NEGROES REARED BY FOES

This verse is directed to the so-called Negroes who were

reared by their enemies, our enemies have never taught us the truth, because the truth is in the Black Man's favor. The truth will free the so-called Negroes from the fear of the enemies (devils) and the truth will destroy the so-called Negroes love and worship of the devils as it has done for my followers and myself.

Allah is Truth. His religion Islam is Truth. White America is not losing time in trying to prevent the so-called Negroes from accepting it, Truth (Islam).

They are so afraid, the so-called Negroes are going over to Islam, that they are even disgracing themselves in their efforts to oppose the truth.

They are now even willing to have intermarriages between the so-called Negroes and white just to prevent the so-called Negroes from accepting the Truth (Islam). As some of the devils have said: "The best way to beat Muhammad is to make democracy work."

TRIBE OF SHABAZZ

Allah is the Greatest; it is incumbent upon Allah (God) to awaken and teach the truth to the mentally dead, lost and found members of the Black Nation from the Tribe of Shabazz (so-called Negroes). Hell was not prepared for any black person. It was prepared for the devils (white race). This, the white race knows. This is why they desire to take every one of you to their doom with them.

No pro-white so-called Negro leadership will work for the good of black people regardless to what.

To speak for the truth, you need a fearless Muslim leader who knows people, their origin and destiny. The so-called Negroes need the unity of all darker people the same as white people seek and have the unity of one another, especially against the non-whites.

The so-called Negroes have millions of members, the Indians and all darker Latin Americans of their own nations. But the so-called Negroes need certain qualification that is very much necessary for them to be respected by any member of their nation. They would even be respected by their enemies I they had self-respect. Being without self-respect, others are unable to respect you.

TRUTH SHALL MAKE YOU FREE

When Jesus prophesied: "The truth shall make you free," He did not tell what this truth was that would make us free. He refused to go into details even after being questioned by the devils who were claiming kinship to Abraham. Later admitted He could not guide them into all the truth. But Jesus, prophesied that the Father (Allah) would send one in His Name who would teach and guide the people into all truth.

This one would only say that which he heard from the father say (getting it directly from the mouth of God). This truth Jesus was referring to is the knowledge of God, the devil and the end of one and the rise of another. This truth Allah (God) has now revealed and it is being preached first to the so-called Negroes and then throughout the world of the Black Nation.

The real danger which now confronts and will destroy the future of the so-called Negroes is the great temptation which the white Christian race is now putting on just for the purpose of trapping the so-called Negroes.

That is their parading their bold, half-nude girls and women before the public along with some of the most filthy and indecent acts that is known to man. They were even more decent when they were savages. Then they did try to hide their nakedness with the skin of beasts. This is the truth! Believe it or leave it!

UNITY

Sincere unity comes from the love of one another and agreement is assured. The lack of unity is the real cause of the existing dissension among the so-called Negroes. There is no love for one another and this lack of love makes it impossible to unite and agree with each other.

Allah, in the Person of Master W.F. Muhammad (God in Person) brought the key to our unity by giving us the knowledge of self and others. This knowledge of self has made us to love self and our kind, not the devil. It is against the law of nature for us to love strange flesh as we love self and kind. Unlike is repelled by alike, though unlike may well attract. But the law of nature will rebel though unlike may well attract against it because of the lack of alikeness. Perfect unity is obtained then from alikeness, and not from unlike. Every kind of life we see in this world is different; everyone unlike, but yet unity is at work among only the alike. We see that the world of mankind is intelligent enough to recognize their own likeness and repel unlikeness. Therefore, they like to own a part of this earth alone to themselves – Black, Brown, Yellow, Red and White. But my poor people who like unlike and hate alike because they have no knowledge of self or kind; not to mention other than self. They are, therefore called blind, deaf and dumb, and this is true even it if is offensive and disgraceful to be called such names.

Love and unity cannot be enjoyed without the knowledge of self and kind. The so-called Negroes should attend the meetings of the Muslims to learn about self and kind as revealed to us by Allah (to whom be praised forever. Who came in the Person of Master W. F. Muhammad, the hoped for and long awaited for the last 2,000 years. The Great Mahdi, the Finder, of us, the Lost and the Last members of the Divine Nation of righteous, the Great Restorer of the Kingdom of Islam.) Every one of us who accepts Allah as our God and His religion, Islam (entire submission to the will of Allah), enjoys
peace of mind, contentment and have no fear nor shall they

grieve. This religion, Islam, is actually powered by Allah (God,) and this power and the great wisdom—the secret of God, and the universe that we live in – automatically invites us.

One of the main purposes of His coming is to unite the Lost and Found members of the Great Asiatic Nation of Islam. His supreme wisdom given to the Lost-Found Nation of Islam, as He calls us, will put us on top of civilization as Yakub's supreme wisdom and knowledge on how to trick the righteous into doing evil – just the opposite of right – put his people, the White Race. The Great Mahdi will make a nation from the product of righteousness and teach them a Supreme knowledge of the God of righteousness that has never been taught since the creation of the universe. He will make his people rule forever, as that wisdom is the utmost Divine knowledge And as I have saith, it is so powerful that it automatically unites us.

Hurry and Join Unto Your Own Kind. The Time of This World is At Hand.

WE MUST BE OURSELVES

We are faced with the choice of accepting self or other than self. The absence of love for self, makes us love other than self; hatred of self keeps us fighting and opposing self. We must do something for self and stop working against each other for the joy of our enemies. We must prepare for tomorrow. We cannot depend on the White race to continue to farm and grow food, cotton and wool to clothe us. We have to get rid of thinking like a child. We have to learn to think and do like men of all other nations and look after our own needs.

We must unite and work together in order to make it easy for all. We must go to school and try to get a college and university education. We must learn **engineering of all kinds, teachership, chemistry, medicine, astronomy** and other sciences such as professions, trades, navigation, etc.

Learn to do for self and nation, what other civilized nations are doing for themselves. Too long we have been lazy. Think in the way of being self-independent. Unite and build a better Black nation, worthy of its name "the first." Speak good for self and kind; never join in making fun of your people with non-members of your people. Never seek to take advantage of your own Black brother or sister. Be true to self and other than your own kind, defend each other against danger to lives and property of your own. Be clean internal as well as external. Stop using tobacco in any form. Stop eating the filthy swine (PIG). Stop being loud in the public and in secret. Stop using filthy language in public and in secret. Stop using drugs and whiskey.

Stop trying to mix with other than your own kind. Stop going to church and go to the Mosque of Islam where you will be loved and respected and protected by the God of Islam and your Nation. Be yourself and fear Allah alone. Do not think the White man is being blessed in not asking you to take part in the third world war or final war of the Western world's civilization. Join onto your own kind and be yourself!

HURRY AND JOIN ONTO YOUR OWN KIND. THE TIME OF THIS WORLD IS AT HAND.

WE MUST HAVE LAND AS OTHER NATIONS

YOU SAY, "BUT I don't want the White man to carry us. Just give us an equal chance." What kind of equal chance? What do twenty million people look like milling around in a factory of White people all the days of their lives and their children's lives, looking for a job? We need to look for some land. Who will recognize millions and millions of people who will not protest their condition? Yours and my condition here in America is the worst of any people on earth—it is unequalled, and we are without one tiny state in the union. We are still demanding equality.

The White man will not accept you as his equal because he knows his slave is not his equal. He does not want you to marry his daughter. He does not want you as his son or his son-in-law even though you greedily desire to be. You are most eager for integration, so you may have a chance of intermixing and intermarrying with them than you are for justice for your people and getting some land—land for you and your children on this earth.

IF I AM YOUR equal as you are a citizen, then prove that I am a citizen of America by giving to me some earth like that which you own. The so-called American Negroes can never have a successful future in America as long as they do not own some earth. You are a nation within a nation. You have been carried by another nation all your life, here, in America for more than four hundred years. Today you continue to beg them to carry you and recognize you as their equal without even asking them for something. You are not asking them for anything worthwhile. Why don't you unite as leaders and go down to Washington and tell the Washington leaders, "We don't want to sit in your schools beside you. What we really want from you, if you don't want to let us go, is a place for our people in this country. You have said that we are free. Let us go! If we are not going and you will not help us to go, then give us a chance to live to ourselves here. We don't want to force our presence on you, and upon your children. If you will not let us go and seek earth somewhere else other than America, then set aside some of these states for us."

THE SO-CALLED AMERICAN Negroes say they don't want to be separated and that is because of their inferior knowledge of their own kind and the White race. If you had a thorough knowledge of the White race, you would desire to be separated. What have the slave-masters done in the way of justice that we should want to live with them? What have they done in the way of justice that we should want to eat with them, drink with them, walk with them or marry them? What have they done for us that make the so-called Negroes desire them. It appears to be their greatest desire to make unity and love to the slave-master's children.

You should first make unity and love among yourselves and your own kind. I think White people would be foolish to accept a so-called Negro as a friend or as a neighbor of theirs, when he is not a friend or neighbor to himself. We are divided. There is no unity among us. We have allowed the slave-master's religion to divide us one hundred percent. We do not have a knowledge of the Whiteman, or ourselves. I have told you the truth.

Some of you say and write that, "Elijah is teaching hate." What is there in the teachings of Elijah Muhammad that you can single out as "hate teaching?" What part or the whole of this teaching do you construe as hate? If I say that you should love yourself as a Black man, is that hate? I say that Black mankind are the people from whom you were taken. Is that hate? I say the White race came after the Black and is a grafted race from the Black man. Is that hate? I am not telling you to hate White people. I am only telling you who they are. We are very quick to single out one of our own as an enemy, when he speaks up for the good of Black mankind. I am for the Black man!

SOME OF YOU may not like me because I love my own kind. Any man that is brown, yellow, red or coal black is a member of the Black nation. Any man who has not accepted self or speak and love others more than his own kind, cannot be trusted. The time has arrived for the truth. You should know the truth. You should not err in this day and time. You should know exactly where you stand. There are no people more blessed this day than the so-called American Negroes, who have been chosen by Allah, Himself, The God of The Universe. You and I should be happy to know today that we have on our side a God who defends and guides us.

You may believe in that which the slave-master gave to you for a religion. But you must prove to me that it was the religion of the prophets. You may say, "the Negro is not mentioned in the bible or any Holy Book." If you don't see where you are mentioned by the name, "Negro," it is only right that you should discard the name. Then see if you can find yourself under some other name. Almighty God, Allah, has taught me the truth to teach to you. I must deliver it to you whether you accept it or not. It is not my fault if you reject it after I offer the truth to you. It is my fault if I don't offer to you the truth God gave to me.

WHAT DAY ARE we living in? We are living in the day of judgment of the Caucasian World. We are living in the day in which we should separate. You must know this even though your minds are filled with wealth, sport and play. It is the time of judgment of this world as you and I have known it. There are scholars who think this is the time of their judgment. Who is going to tell you, if one of your own kind does not? Are you looking again for a spirit God to come and peer out of the clouds of heaven and tell you? That does not happen! When you do see someone come, they will not be coming to teach and school, but to execute justice. The religion of Islam is the only salvation for my people.

WE MUST HAVE MORE THAN A JOB

The condition and history of my people, the so-called Negro in America, is pitiful and a disgrace before civilized peoples of the earth. We have nothing of our own. We can only say we have what the slave-master and his children have given us. It is a foolish idea to depend on the White man to care for us and our ever-increasing population. The leaders of the Nation of the Black man in America must get this foolish idea out of their heads and quick!

I think the American White man has done a good job, in a manner of speaking, in caring for us one hundred years, after he has said to our fathers that we were free. We have not exercised that freedom, nor have we asked the rulers of the land to let us go for ourselves. We have not said to the slave-master, "Take that which belongs to you and let us have that which you have taken from us." Instead, we have acted as a lazy man. My people have constantly asked the White man to give, give, give. Their cry has been of pleading and begging. To the slave-master has been said, "I want the love and friendship of you who have enslaved my fathers, not the love of my own kind."

This is the prevailing idea of the leadership of the so-called American Negro. Their craving is to be made like their slave-master and his children. "Let me be like them. Let me be the brother or sister of White America." They ask this before they even love their own kind. We have been craving for the love of other than our own kind. It is an act of which we should be ashamed. It is an act of craving that is disgracing you and your children. It is an act that keeps you a slave and causes criticism by the civilized nations of the earth.

I desire that you think along the terms of Elijah Muhammad. The so-called Negro must be separated from his slave-master and his children. He must be given the chance to build a nation for himself. He must be given the chance to go for self. The so-called Negro is four hundred years behind with a history in the Western Hemisphere written in hard labor, injustice and blood.

We have always been ready to jump to our feet and defend the slave-master against his enemies.

For those lost lives and efforts, we have nothing today. My people have become a nation of beggars. We only beg the master for a job. We want sport and play on an equal basis with the rich White man of America. The country belongs to the White man who took it from the red Indian. All we have asked for is a job. Then we give the paycheck back to the White paymaster. We keep five dollars to sit in a show or a game of sport and play. The bible states we are a foolish people.

You must get out of such foolish acts! You must unite and help me! Regardless of your fear of the slave-master and his children, you must unite with me. We have before us, a job that must be done! We must care for and deliver our people. Our people are crying for freedom, moaning for justice and calling for equality to be free to integrate, intermarry or mix the blood, as this is already going on. It is a disgrace before the nations of the earth.

Almighty God, Allah, is in our midst today to bring the so-called American Negro out of the hands of the slave-master just as He delivered Moses and his people out of the hands of Pharaoh from a four-hundred- year period of bondage.

HURRY and join onto your own kind. The time of this world is at hand.

WHAT IS UN-AMERICAN?

According to the dictionary's definition of un-American, it means: "one that is not American; not characteristic of or proper to America, foreign or opposed to the American character, usages, standard, etc."

As you know, any or all Negroes that seek freedom, justice and equality, is or are charged or accused of being un-American. They are accused with seeking to overthrow the government of America by force. (We, Muslims, prohibit the carrying of arms, yet we are accused of planning to overthrow the government by force). No Negro leader has been successful in helping his people to freedom, justice and equality, that was not opposed by both his own people and the merciless, wicked White Americans.

Also, by those poison intellectual so-called Negroes who love and worship the devils and hate self and kind. Today, the Americans hope to unite all educated so-called Negroes, along with their already poisoned Negro Christian Preachers, against we the Muslims that preach freedom, justice and equality for the Black Nation. They are united against my followers and I. Thanks be to Allah, you are a little late to win. Allah (God) knew the tricks that you would use to try deceiving the Black Man before you were created.

UN-AMERICAN: I wish to prove, according to the English language in this article, that every so-called Negro, Indian, and all non-White Europeans, are un-American according to the dictionary's definition of an American. An American, according to the dictionary, "is a citizen of the United States or of the earlier British Colonies: one not belonging to one of the aboriginal races. (We belong to the aboriginal nation of the earth; the White or European race is not aboriginal). 2. Native or inhabitant of the Western Hemisphere.
The above explanation makes it clear that we are not

members of the White Europeans, nor descendants of that race. We are the aboriginal un-Americans. The above explanation also makes it clear that we (so-called Negroes) are not, and cannot be American citizens, since we are not American by nature, nor by race. A true American is one other than the aboriginal race or races that inhabited the Western Hemisphere, or the whole Planet Earth, before the coming of the White man from Europe. We, the so-called Negroes (members of the aboriginal people of the Earth, and of the tribe of Shabazz) were kidnapped from our native land and people by the White Englishmen and Americans.

We were brought here not to be made Americans, nor American citizens; but rather, to be slaves or servants for the true American citizens; —Whites, who originally came from Europe. We, descendants of the Asiatic Nation from the continent of Africa, after 100 years of so-called freedom, cannot claim by the law of justice, to be Americans or American citizens. We are un-American and by nature, we are different. Know from this day on, that if you are a so-called Negro, red, black, or an Indian, or any member of the aboriginal Black Nation, you are an un-American. Even though you may have been born in the United States of America, you cannot be an American.

USED FOR CRIMINAL PURPOSES: What, or why are we called un-American? It is to classify us as criminals, or with crimes that we are not guilty of. They make the truth God has given to us untruth; they use it to conceal our true intentions. But at the same time, they claim freedom of speech, freedom of the press and religious freedom lawful under the Constitution. Again, it is abundantly clear to you that have eyes, that the Americans never intended freedom for their so-called Negroes. She stands in the way and opposes true freedom, justice and equality from coming to the poor Black man and woman in the Western Hemisphere. She is pleased with the foolish and ignorant worship of the so-called Negroes. She doesn't ever want the Negroes to accept the true religion, which is Islam. WHY? Here (In Islam) the Negroes have a true God and true friends on his side, and that means help to the poor Negroes against his open enemies, the White race.

So, YOU CAN SEE, or you will see why they do not want a so-called Negro Muslim people in America. It means independence, friendship, Divine guidance and help against the devils. As it is written in the Holy Qur'an, "know that Allah is with the Muslims."

TRICK THE NEGROES TO STAY IN DEVIL'S NAMES: For the first time, the so-called Negroes are awakening to just why White Americans still like to call their much hated and despised, once Negro slaves, after their names; or make the Negroes think names do not mean anything that they should remain in them. The devils have knowledge of the time. They know you will not be accepted by God, nor your own nation if represented under their names, which are not names of God—and will not see the Hereafter. The intellectual so-called Negroes think it is a disgrace to them to not be called by the slave master's name; and if I wanted to be called "Muhammad," I should go to court and have my name changed legally.

I laughed and said, I'm sorry, I have my legal name; there is no law to make me pay to be called by my legal name. I have been called by an illegal name. Now, I have gotten rid of that illegal slave name for a legal and Holy Name of God. Again, we must remember, the White race never intended anything like good for you. They are not seeking good for you today; death is really their aim for you. Why do they oppose our struggle for justice and freedom if they want to see all people free and in unity? They are not referring to you; you are not people in their eyes; it is their people they are referring to.

Why do they oppose separation of us into a state or territory of our own, since we cannot live in peace with them? When we read of the evils done to us and to our fathers by this race of devils, we cannot foresee anything in them but evil, hatred and murder for us and to our unborn children.

Read some of their books on what went on against our slave

parents by the fathers of these modern murderers of ours. For instance, the book entitled, "Brown Americans," by Edwin R. Embree, printed 1946, page 54, tells the story of laws against education for the so-called Negroes. He quotes a devil, Henry Berry, as saying while speaking in the Virginia House of Delegates, in 1832, describing the situation as existed at that time in many parts of the South: "We have, as far as possible, closed every avenue by which light may enter the slaves' minds ... (The avenue of the light of Allah you are unable to shut out from coming to us). ... If we could extinguish the capacity to see the light, our work would be complete; they would then be on a level with the beasts of the field and we should be safe. I am not certain that we would not do it, if we could find out the process and that on the plea of necessity."

The above words, desires and works against you, are still in the hearts of their evil blood-thirsty children against you. Today, they go around in large cities like Chicago, at night, in cars, loaded with baseball bats, guns, iron pipes and knives to pounce, upon and kill poor, harmless, so-called Negroes. We are living under the very shadow of death in such a place as America.

Unity under the guidance and protection of Allah will bring an end to this horrible situation. What do you see as a future in them for you and your children, nothing but hell? Remember, if you are Black, or a member of the Black Nation, you are un-American. If you want equal justice and a decent way of life to live, or have love for the Black people, you are un-American. The American is the only one that can sing, "The Land of the Free"—it is for the White Americans.

WHAT THE SO-CALLED NEGRO MUST DO

All over the earth today, we see men coming into unity, oneness, or solidarity. The European Nations are in a bond or pact referred to as NATO or the Warsaw Pact. They are attempting to establish a European Common Market. In Africa, there is the Organization of Arab States and much work is going on toward uniting all the people of Africa. In the United Nations, those nations which have something in common or identical people, traits, culture or borders are ... groups or blocs. Men everywhere are seeking unity among themselves. Every race of people want unity with their own kind first, except my people, the so-called Negro in America.

Our condition and lack of love for ourselves must be attributed to the slave-master. He has been our teacher until the coming of Almighty God, Allah. The slave-master has robbed my people of their God, religion, name, language and culture. They are now deaf, dumb and blind to the knowledge of self.

The worst kind of crime has been committed against us for we were robbed of our desire to even want to think and do for self. We are often pictured by the slave-master as a lazy and trifling people who are without thoughts of advancement. I say, this is a condition which the slave-master very cleverly wanted and created within and among the so-called Negro.

Robert H. Kinzer and Edward Sagarin, in their book, "The Negro in American Business," Page 81, state that the history of America would be different today if the slaves, freed from bondage had been given, in addition to the three amendments to the Constitution, the famous "forty acres and a mule." The slaves instead started not only without land and the money to purchase it, but with few avenues open to earn and save such money. Ownership of producing land is a prime and necessary part of freedom. A people cannot exist freely without land, and the so-called Negro in land ownership or limiting the areas in which such purchases or even rentals could be made. Are you not left restricted to the poorer sections the slave-master is abandoning throughout America?

Again, Mr. Kinzer and Mr. Sagarin give a hint in their book of the great psychological strategy of the slave-master on his slave—that is the original brainwash. On page 84, the authors state that the land sold to the slave was of poor quality and in an inferior location. They state, the so-called Negro faced pressure against his becoming a farm owner and pressure from the White community that he remain a tenant.

We encountered credit difficulties, hardships of repayment of loans, and hardship with White executives from whom the loans must be asked. All of this is part of the clever plan to discourage my people from wanting to own producing land for themselves and to cause a great dislike, within them for having anything to do with tilling, cultivating, extracting and producing for themselves as other free and independent people. It is a shame! This shows you and me what White America is to us, and just why we have not been able to do anything worthwhile for self. They want us to be helpless, so they can mistreat us as always. We must come together and unite. IT IS TIME.

I think it is a disgrace for us to be satisfied with only a servant's part. We should and must, as other people, want for ourselves what other civilized nations have! Let us do for ourselves that which we are begging the slave-master to do for us. Do not be fooled by the false promises of civil rights and the softening of their language. It is offered to you now to keep you from becoming free of their evil plans of depriving you of the offer made to us by Allah—if we would submit to Him, He will set us in heaven at once. It is only justice that we be given land and provisions for a start so, we may do for ourselves. This is what the other new emerging nations are given. We want good productive land; not earth that is scorched, but land that would produce crops and hold foundations for structures.

Let us make this clear, I am not begging, for if it pleases Allah, He will give us a home and I am with Him. Today, according to Allah's (God's) word, we are living in a time of THE GREAT SEPARATION of the Blacks and the Whites. The prophesied 400 years of slavery, which the so-called Negroes would serve White people, ended in 1955. The so-called Negroes must return to their own. Nothing else will solve their problem. The Divine Power is working and will continue to work in favor of the so-called Negroes' return to their own. The separation would be a blessing for both sides. It was the only solution according to the Bible for Israel and the Egyptians; it will prove to be the only solution for America and her slaves.

INDEX

Abraham, 56, 64, 76, 77, 78, 79, 80, 82, 86, 92, 94, 110, 112, 113, 140, 207, 212, 262, 265

Africa, 132, 134, 135, 136, 143, 152, 166, 167, 183, 184, 191, 235, 251, 258, 276, 279

Allah: Wallace Fard Muhammad, 35, 36, 97, 137, 140, 162, 185, 206, 211, 226, 236, 252, 263, 284; Mahdi, 17, 26, 91, 104, 137, 140, 252, 263, 266, 267

Asia, 37, 38, 40, 50, 60, 134, 135, 136, 143, 166, 167, 183, 191, 235, 237, 251

believer, 30, 59, 78, 95, 102, 104, 152, 188, 244, 250

Bible, 19, 21, 22, 25, 26, 30, 39, 54, 57, 66, 71, 74, 76, 77, 80, 81, 82, 83, 86, 88, 89, 91, 92, 95, 97, 98, 99, 101, 102, 107, 108, 109, 110, 113, 117, 119, 120, 122, 147, 149, 152, 156, 159, 184, 186, 197, 199, 201, 212, 217, 220, 233, 236, 237, 238, 261, 281

Buddhism, 67

Christ, 26, 77, 85, 86, 196, 226, 284

do for self, 174, 228, 268, 279

education, 82, 124, 128, 134, 169, 170, 173, 174, 175, 176, 177, 215, 224, 268, 278

Elder Lightfoot Solomon Michaux, 227

Europe, 37, 38, 40, 47, 48, 50, 71, 81, 85, 142, 143, 145, 167, 210, 221, 232, 237, 249, 276

farm, 131, 258, 268, 280

fear, 21, 62, 63, 64, 67, 102, 104, 115, 116, 131, 143, 147, 151, 152, 161, 181, 183, 190, 201, 203, 208, 209, 211, 215, 227, 234, 240, 242, 255, 263, 264, 266, 268, 274

Government, 30, 64, 66, 117, 146, 209, 235

history, v, 19, 21, 34, 40, 47, 77, 81, 85, 91, 110, 119, 133, 138, 141, 145, 149, 152, 167, 170, 175, 185, 190, 191, 192, 203, 207, 209, 211, 218, 220, 227, 233, 238, 249, 255, 273, 279

Indians, 17, 48, 63, 130, 178, 207, 216, 253, 265

Islands, 63, 166

Israel, 90, 102, 119, 152, 154, 184, 214, 218, 226, 247, 250, 281

Jesus, v, 22, 25, 26, 34, 56, 57, 63, 64, 70, 71, 76, 77, 78, 81, 82, 83, 85, 86, 88, 89, 90, 91, 92, 94, 95, 97, 98, 99, 101, 102, 106, 108, 112, 118, 119, 122, 134, 140, 146, 149, 151, 153, 154, 178, 196, 226, 229, 232, 236, 243, 255, 261, 262, 265

Jews, 34, 57, 58, 77, 78, 80, 83, 89, 91, 92, 99, 154, 166

Los Angeles, California: Los Angeles, iii, 126, 127, 196

Major Donald Keyhoe, 153, 160

Martin Luther King, 218, 227, 228, 232

Mecca, 25, 27, 29, 34, 108, 112, 146, 148, 149

Monroe, Louisiana, 141, 142, 194, 243

Moses, 38, 41, 42, 43, 47, 50, 56, 59, 64, 70, 76, 77, 78, 81, 82, 83, 85, 86, 92, 94, 99, 101, 102, 106, 112, 118, 119, 132, 133, 140, 152, 153, 218, 220, 226, 227, 229, 233, 236, 243, 247, 255, 261, 262, 274

Mosque, 102, 142, 194, 225, 268

Mother Plane, 149, 160

Nkrumah, 174

Pelan, 30, 33, 36

police, 141, 142, 194, 196, 237

Prayer, 103, 104

preachers, 54, 82, 107, 109, 110, 116, 120, 136, 178, 196, 203, 215, 218, 226, 227, 228, 242, 243, 248

president, 219

prophecy, 22, 88, 91, 118, 119, 124, 145, 146, 150, 167, 171, 207, 236

Qur'an, 78, 79, 81, 82, 86, 87, 89, 91, 92, 94, 95, 100, 101, 102, 104, 106, 107, 109, 110, 112, 114, 115, 119, 121, 133, 152, 153, 156, 159, 161, 162, 173, 191, 212, 213, 217, 226, 231, 233, 234, 235, 236, 237, 243, 252, 255, 256, 260, 261, 277

Rev. George C. Violenes, 77, 81, 82, 83, 85, 86, 88, 89, 90, 100, 101, 107, 109

revelation, 39, 86

Robert H. Kinzer, 279, 280

savage, 40, 41, 96, 207

Senator Arthur R. Gottschalk, 238, 239

Shabazz, 60, 115, 151, 180, 186, 196, 207, 251, 257, 264, 276

slave code, 216

The Wheel, 153, 158, 159

unity, 36, 59, 73, 98, 128, 130, 131, 132, 140, 164, 169, 173, 175, 184, 207, 222, 223, 225, 250, 253, 264, 266, 271, 277, 279

William Goodell, 216

women, v, 39, 52, 73, 121, 142, 164, 178, 203, 221, 237, 251, 265

Yakub, 23, 25, 26, 27, 28, 29, 30, 31, 32, 33, 36, 38, 40, 41, 46, 75, 95, 155, 255, 260, 267

GRATITUDE

All Praise Is Due To Allah, Who Came In The Person of Master W. Fard Muhammad. We thank Him for raising from among us His Messenger Messiah and Christ, the Most Honored and Honorable Elijah Muhammad. We thank them both for the Honorable Minister Louis Farrakhan. I would like to thank the believers who have lent their talent and skill in the completion of An Invincible Truth Volume II. Gratitude and Appreciation to Sis. Donna Muhammad of Memphis, TN; Sis. Letitia Muhammad of Detroit, MI; Sis. Marcella X of Chicago, IL and Bro. Jahleel Muhammad of Detroit, MI